Comments on other *Amazing Stories* from readers & reviewers

"Tightly written volumes filled with lots of wit and humour about famous and infamous Canadians."
Eric Shackleton, *The Globe and Mail*

"The heightened sense of drama and intrigue, combined with a good dose of human interest is what sets Amazing Stories *apart."*
Pamela Klaffke, *Calgary Herald*

"This is popular history as it should be... For this price, buy two and give one to a friend."
Terry Cook, a reader from Ottawa, on **Rebel Women**

"Glasner creates the moment of the explosion itself in graphic detail...she builds detail upon gruesome detail to create a convincingly authentic picture."
Peggy McKinnon, *The Sunday Herald,* on **The Halifax Explosion**

"It was wonderful...I found I could not put it down. I was sorry when it was completed."
Dorothy F. from Manitoba on **Marie-Anne Lagimodière**

"Stories are rich in description, and bristle with a clever, stylish realness."
Mark Weber, *Central Alberta Advisor,* on **Ghost Town Stories II**

"A compelling read. Bertin...has selected only the most intriguing tales, which she narrates with a wealth of detail."
Joyce Glasner, *New Brunswick Reader,* on **Strange Events**

"The resulting book is one readers will want to share with all the women in their lives."
Lynn Martel, *Rocky Mountain Outlook,* on **Women Explorers**

EAST COAST MURDERS

EAST COAST MURDERS

Mysteries, Crimes, and Scandals

CRIME/MYSTERY

by Allison Finnamore

To Debby,
for being such a truly remarkable person

PUBLISHED BY ALTITUDE PUBLISHING CANADA LTD.
1500 Railway Avenue, Canmore, Alberta T1W 1P6
www.altitudepublishing.com
1-800-957-6888

Extreme care has been taken to ensure that all information presented in
this book is accurate and up to date. Neither the author nor the
publisher can be held responsible for any errors.

Publisher	Stephen Hutchings
Associate Publisher	Kara Turner
Editor	Lori Burwash
Digital Photo Colouring	Bryan Pezzi

We acknowledge the financial support of the Government
of Canada through the Book Publishing Industry Development
Program (BPIDP) for our publishing activities.

Altitude GreenTree Program
Altitude Publishing will plant twice as many trees as were used
in the manufacturing of this product.

National Library of Canada Cataloguing in Publication Data

Finnamore, Allison
East Coast murders / Allison Finnamore.

(Amazing stories)
ISBN 1-55439-027-3

1. Murder--Atlantic Provinces. I. Title. II. Series: Amazing stories (Calgary, Alta.)

HV6535.C32A85 2005   364.152'3'09715   C2005-902839-4

Amazing Stories® is a registered trademark of Altitude Publishing Canada Ltd.

Printed and bound in Canada by Friesens
2 4 6 8 9 7 5 3 1

Contents

Prologue

Harry Flohr was backed into a corner. He desperately wanted no part of the mutiny that was about to start. But Gustav Rau, Flohr's shipmate and the leader of the plan, had decided otherwise. When Flohr told Rau he wouldn't take part, the leader was unequivocal: become part of the mutiny or die.

Flohr shuddered to think of the bloodiness that lay ahead, but he knew his fate was sealed. He knew he had to garner enough courage to surface onto the deck of the Veronica *and slit a man's throat, as Rau had ordered.*

Trying to muster himself, Flohr was still below deck when Rau and Willem Smith came hunting for him. Both men were enraged. Smith had been distracting the intended victim, waiting for Flohr to arrive wielding the knife. But Flohr had taken too long, and Smith had run out of patience.

This time, under the watchful eyes of Rau and Smith, Flohr went up on deck. Then he looked on in horror as Rau struck a shipmate over the head with an iron fastener. He stifled the vomit that rose to his throat as the man's blood sprayed over their clothes and the body crumpled to the deck.

Flohr was trapped on a ship on the brink of rebellion. The bloodshed had only just begun.

Chapter 1
A Mother's Madness

eing a mother to her eight children came naturally to Minnie McGee. Everyone in St. Mary's Road knew the petite woman was a patient, loving, caring mother. So devoted to the children, Minnie hardly ever let them out of her sight. She rarely even left the yard, so she could be close to them. That she was capable of killing them was the furthest thought from anyone's mind.

When two of her children became seriously ill in the winter of 1911, Minnie was understandably concerned. Whatever severe infection plagued their small bodies, they were unable to ward it off and, in January 1912, succumbed to the sickness.

Distraught, Minnie never seemed to recover from the

loss. Known for her patience, after the deaths, Minnie began to fly into fits of rage with little or no provocation and became increasingly introverted. She barely left the house and ignored neighbourly greetings. Everyone dismissed her actions as her way of mourning the deaths of the children.

Her husband, Patrick, likely wasn't much help. There were rumours he abused Minnie on the rare occasions that he was home. As a labourer, he had to travel where the jobs took him, to fishing boats, sawmills, or factories. He was sometimes on the road for several months at a time.

In April, Minnie was home alone with her six children after Patrick had taken a factory job in another community. Since she now avoided leaving her house, she would send her children to the store for supplies, so it wasn't unusual when she asked 10-year-old Johnny to run and get some matches. As a treat for doing the errand, she told him he could buy some candy.

Johnny came home clutching the candy and two boxes of matches, a total of 100. He didn't notice when his mother placed just the very tips of the matches in a small bowl of water. Nor did he notice when she later tossed the bare sticks into the wood stove but kept the clear liquid. Like the other children, Johnny went about playing, trying to keep out of trouble. He kept right on playing until his uncle came to get him, needing help with some farm chores. Off they went, leaving just before supper.

Supper that night for the rest of the children was herring,

cornmeal bread, and tea — common fare for the family. Except, this night, a toxic brew had been mixed into the children's food.

The next day, Thursday, April 11, 13-year-old Louis, 12-year-old Penzie, 8-year-old George, 6-year-old Bridget, and 5-year-old Thomas were complaining of stomach cramps and were terribly sleepy, but were still well enough to play in the yard. With Johnny still away, Minnie sent Penzie to the store for additional matches, telling her to leave word on the way for Johnny to come right home.

Armed with the matches, the mother prepared more poison to give to her children. Johnny never did come home that night, staying on at his uncle's farm, where he was still needed for chores.

On Friday, Minnie decided it was time to call for a doctor — her children were desperately ill. By the time the doctor got there, three were already dead. When Patrick arrived later that evening, he and a second doctor desperately attempted to save the last two children. But within 24 hours, all five were dead.

Because of the symptoms, the physicians quickly determined that poisoning, perhaps from decaying fish they ate for supper the night before, was the cause of death.

On Saturday, Minnie demanded that Johnny return home with her. She wanted him nearby — it was almost time to bury his brothers and sisters. Johnny did come home, and later that day, he and his parents attended the wake for his siblings. The whole community turned out to express condolences over the tragic loss, each person trying to comprehend how such a dreadful thing could happen.

Thomas McCarron was at the wake. He lived near the McGees and knew, like everyone else, how dedicated Minnie was to her children. But Thomas was a policeman, too, and knew the look of a killer. Sitting in the church near the family, Thomas was gazing around the room when his eyes came to rest on Minnie. His heart leaped as he saw in her the unmistakable signs of a murderer.

Invisible to the untrained eye, the characteristics were glaringly obvious to Thomas. He could see it in her eyes, in the way she tilted her head, in the way she clasped her hands together on her lap. Minute details easily overlooked by most were, for Thomas, telltale signs. His problem was, Minnie was such a nurturing mother, how would he convince others to help him investigate the unlikely suspect?

Thomas decided to talk to Minnie, to explore his suspicions and determine if it really was a killer's look that he had seen. Keep it casual, he thought, just see how she's doing.

It was an irrational, difficult conversation. Minnie was obviously devastated by the deaths. She even mentioned taking her own life. Little else she said to the policeman made sense. Friends and neighbours said Minnie was consumed with grief. Thomas wondered if it wasn't insanity that had consumed her psyche.

Fearing for Johnny's safety under his mother's care, the

officer approached the town's doctors, expressing his concerns, suspicions, and observations. Like Thomas, they were curious. One doctor arranged to have the body of one of the children exhumed. Aside from pinpointing exactly what had caused the deaths of the five children, there was little else the doctors could do except keep an eye on Johnny and Minnie.

Thomas also approached several of Minnie's nearby relatives, trying to get one of them to believe even a bit of his suspicion. The policeman wanted to get Johnny out of the McGee home and into a safe shelter. But Minnie's relatives could see only her grief, not her guilt. The last thing they wanted to do was take away her one surviving child. A few people, though, did agree to keep an eye out for the boy and check in on him occasionally.

It was the best Thomas could hope for. At least the boy's father was still home.

Whether Patrick returned to work out of a duty to care for the remainder of his family or whether Minnie pushed him out the door, anxious to be rid of him, is unclear. Patrick said later that it wasn't his decision — Minnie had told him to go. "I was not the boss," Patrick stated. Regardless, on Monday, Patrick went back to work in a community far from home, only a few days after his five children had died.

With Patrick gone, Thomas had to work harder than ever to gather evidence against Minnie and convince other authorities that Johnny should not be alone in his mother's care.

Meanwhile, at the McGee home, Minnie needed more

matches. This time, she told Johnny to walk a different way, to another store.

Two days later, the boy was so ill Minnie rushed to a neighbour for help. Minnie was sick, too, and they urgently needed a doctor, she claimed. By the time the physician arrived, Johnny's sickness had eased a bit and Minnie's symptoms had disappeared completely.

The boy's sudden illness and his symptoms lent credibility to Thomas's concerns. The doctor began to think that maybe Minnie did have something to do with her children's death. Just in case, he stopped at several homes, asking neighbours to check in on Minnie and Johnny. The neighbours agreed and the men took turns sitting with the mother and boy.

During the visits, Minnie barely made sense and would often sit for long periods saying nothing at all. Everyone continued to attribute her strange behaviour to the grief she must be suffering.

When the doctor arrived on Friday to check on the boy, there was no change, so he sent for his colleague. Despite his instructions that Minnie not give Johnny anything to eat or drink, she ignored him, slipping her son some warm milk as she diverted the doctor's attention. The doctor, although beginning to show some support for Thomas's theory, apparently still couldn't believe Minnie was killing her own offspring.

After conferring, the community's two doctors agreed that whatever had afflicted Johnny's brothers and sisters was now causing the boy the same problems. It was the final conclusion they needed — they now whole-heartedly believed that Minnie was responsible for her children's deaths. Wrapping Johnny in blankets, they prepared to carry him out.

Minnie fell to pieces. She attempted to stop the doctors from taking her last child, blocking their path. The physicians were insistent, though. They knew the boy couldn't stay with his mother. Pushing past a frenzied Minnie, the doctors carried Johnny to the wagon and took him to the safety of his grandfather's house.

Unfortunately, the doctors had reached their conclusion too late — Johnny died during the night.

It was now clear that Minnie had orchestrated her children's deaths. An inquest was held to discover more about how the young lives were taken. That's when investigators tallied how many matches Minnie's children had bought in the days before their deaths. One report says that Minnie had spent 21¢ on matches — more than 3,000 of the deadly sticks.

Minnie took the stand during the inquest and told a disjointed story. She changed her tale several times, pointing the finger to bad fish, rotten candy, and rancid oatmeal for poisoning her children. The jury concluded that the six McGee children had died from "poisoning of some form," but drew no conclusion as to who had administered the deadly concoction.

The inquest also involved autopsies on some of the

bodies. The bodies of the two children who had died in the winter, apparently from an infection, were dug up, but autopsies confirmed they had indeed died of a virus. Since Johnny's symptoms were the same as his five siblings, the autopsy was performed on his remains — the earlier approval to exhume one of the other children was never carried out. Toxicology exams revealed tissue damage consistent with phosphorous poisoning.

Three days later, on April 26, Minnie McGee was arrested for the murder of her son Johnny. Three months later, a grand jury found there was enough evidence to send the woman to trial.

During the trial, the Crown prosecutor wondered if Minnie was indeed insane. Friends and family testified that Minnie's state of mind gradually deteriorated after the two children died early in the year. By the time the rest of her children started feeling sick, most of what she said and did was strange, they said.

Whatever mental illness or strain Minnie was suffering, she was logical and articulate when she took the stand in her own defence — a complete turnaround from her conduct at the inquest. She explained there was a simple, logical reason her children had died. She had accidentally poisoned them.

So determined was Minnie in giving a believable performance on the witness stand that she didn't even change the expression on her face as she contradicted each Crown witness. For instance, she claimed she went through so many matches because visitors to her home used them or took them when they left. But each of the guests testified they had used their own matches when visiting the McGee home. They had no idea where all those matches had gone.

Once all the evidence had been presented and witnesses called, Minnie's jury was given the option of finding the mother guilty, not guilty, or not guilty by reason of insanity. They quickly returned with a guilty verdict.

The next day, in a short statement passed to the jail doctor, Minnie confessed to killing six of her children. Her only reason was that she had been "feeling very poorly."

In seemingly another plea for help, the next day, during her sentencing hearing, Minnie tried to blame her actions on her husband. Patrick knew she was sick, she told the judge, and knew she was incapable of taking care of their children. Still, he left the children in her care and went off to his jobs around the province. He should have taken steps to ensure the children's safety, Minnie stated.

While sounding quite reasonable up to that point, Minnie fell apart upon hearing her death sentence. She begged to be hanged at that moment, becoming hysterical as she was led from the courtroom.

After her trial, both the Crown prosecutor and defence lawyer agreed they would have been satisfied with a verdict of insanity. Unfortunately, the jurors couldn't understand that Minnie likely wasn't in her right mind when she committed the crimes. Fortunately, the province's justice minister reviewed the case and recognized Minnie's unstable condition. He accepted the defence of insanity and dismissed the death sentence. Instead, he sentenced the woman to life in prison at Kingston Penitentiary in Ontario.

But prison wasn't the place for Minnie to receive the aid she needed. Over the next 16 years, her mental condition deteriorated. Finally, on October 1, 1928, she was moved to the Falconwood Insane Asylum in Charlottetown. There, with more appropriate care, Minnie appeared to improve.

Over time, Minnie became a productive patient. In fact, she was doing so well that, when her father fell ill with mental health problems in 1934, she was granted a release to look after him. After his death, she returned to the asylum, where she died on January 7, 1953.

Chapter 2
Crime of Passion

aced with the unexpected prospect of fatherhood, 20-year-old William Millman was scared. He wasn't ready to settle down and start a family. Everyone in Irishtown-Margate knew he liked to date several women at the same time. It also wasn't a secret that he liked his rum and enjoyed going to dances, taking a turn at the fiddle as the evening grew late. William knew it was too soon for him to be a father. So did everyone else.

But that didn't change the fact that one of his former flings, Mary Tuplin, was claiming she was pregnant and that he was the father. William was aghast by the rumour that was making its way through the Prince Edward Island community in late June. Still, he was curious. He hadn't seen Mary around for months and did wonder if there was any truth to the story.

It was possible, he supposed. They'd met at his friend's house on New Year's Eve and had danced. Just before midnight, when the music stopped, William had held Mary's hand. The kiss they shared as 1887 began made time stand still for both of them, William recalled. It was sweet and lingering, a kiss that held the promise of something more.

Their second date was far more intense. It was only a few days into the New Year when William arrived at Mary's. Her whole family was standing on the porch waiting to meet him. Although unnerving, he managed to make it through the meal. William stayed until Mary's younger brothers and sisters were in bed. He stayed after her parents went to bed. William recalled the intimacy he and Mary shared once they were alone in the family's living room. He would have stayed longer had Mary's father not hollered down the stairs, telling her to get to bed.

So, yes, it was possible that Mary was pregnant and that he was the father. William just didn't want to admit it, even to himself. He was also a bit ashamed. He'd never bothered to call on Mary again after that night.

Finding out the truth about Mary's condition was going to be tricky. They were in a small village, after all. William decided the best thing to do would be to ask a friend from church. William knew that Tom Bryenton and his wife were good friends with the Tuplins. Surely Tom would know.

It took all his courage to approach Tom and ask him if the rumours were true. When the man confirmed that was indeed the story going around town, William was panic-stricken.

But wait. Tom had confirmed there was a rumour travelling about town, but was there any truth to the rumour itself? Was Mary really pregnant? Did she really think he was the father? The Bryentons were going to the Tuplins later that night, Tom told William. His wife could quietly talk to Mary and find out what was going on.

Relieved at the chance to find out the truth, William agreed to the plan. The next few hours passed in a blur.

Meanwhile, the Bryentons were at the Tuplins lending their moral support to the family. One of Mary's brothers was desperately sick and not expected to recover. As the men talked quietly outside the boy's room and Mary's mother fussed in the kitchen, Bryenton's wife took Mary aside. The young woman confirmed the rumours. All of them were true, she said. Yes, she was pregnant. Yes, William was the father. Yes, she was sure.

Upon hearing this news, William was more frightened than ever.

A few hours after Mary confided her secrets, her brother died.

Two days later, after attending the burial, Mary wanted to get away from the house for a while. Before abruptly walking out the door, she had been cradling her sister's newborn baby. The family let her be, knowing she was dealing with a lot in her life. However, when she failed to return after several hours, they became worried.

Mary's father, John, searched late into the night for his daughter but failed to find her. Collapsing in bed after an emotionally exhausting day, he managed to rest for a few hours before rising early the next morning to resume the search.

When Mary's handkerchief, stitched with a fanciful "M" in the corner, was found along the shore of the South West River, John feared something might be dreadfully wrong. Suspicion that she had been murdered grew when it was also discovered that a 45-kilogram rock was missing from an oyster boat tied near William Millman's family's home.

Because of the missing rock, it was assumed that Mary's body had been weighed down and was lying at the bottom of the river. As searchers dragged the river for a body, the rumours that had been swirling about William and Mary's relationship quickly turned into a storm of accusations. Everyone was quick to link William with the girl's death, especially John, who complained loudly to his neighbours about William's brief fling with Mary.

William was petrified by the allegations of murder. He stayed around the village for as long as he could while the search for Mary's body was on, but it wasn't easy. Dragging continued for six days. All the while, rumours ran rampant. The island newspapers and their readers relished every word.

Unable to stand the waiting and the blaming any longer, William left the community. He had never been to Charlottetown and decided the visit was overdue. While there, he planned to talk to a lawyer about the accusations

Mary's father was slinging at him.

The day he left, July 4, Mary's body was found at the bottom of the river. She had been shot twice in the head. The missing rock from the oyster boat was tied around her waist. An autopsy later confirmed she was six months' pregnant.

Sheriffs were ready for William when he returned from Charlottetown on July 5. When police knocked on the door of his family's home, the young man was outwardly calm. He went without a fight, seemingly resigned to facing the consequences of the girl's death.

The preliminary hearing was held July 7, just days after Mary's body was found, but it was several more months before William was tried in front of a jury for the death of Mary Tuplin. In the meantime, he sat in the Queens County Jail in Charlottetown.

On January 24, 1888, a little more than a year after William and Mary had given in to their passion, William's trial began. He could provide little defence and there was ample evidence to implicate him in Mary's death.

William's close friend, Francis Power, gave some of the most damning testimony. He said William had borrowed his loaded pistol before Mary was even missing. When the weapon was returned after her disappearance, two bullets were gone.

Power's brother recounted how William had asked him to lie and testify they were together when Mary disappeared. A 13-year-old neighbour also helped seal William's fate.

Dorothy Adams testified that she was herding home her cows the night Mary vanished when she saw William tie up a boat near Mary's home and walk toward the Tuplin house.

William scrambled to provide an explanation for prosecution's evidence. During the trial, which lasted almost two weeks, his lawyer argued William didn't have time to kill Mary and dispose of her body in the time the other witnesses said. But during the judge's closing address to the jury, he plainly stated he didn't believe the cover-up story. Three hours later, on February 6, William was found guilty of murder.

The fear, worry, and trauma of the last several months finally caught up with William. When he heard the verdict, he fainted and had to be taken from the courtroom to be revived. When he returned for sentencing, the frightened young man stuck his fingers in his ears to avoid hearing his death sentence.

For whatever reason, the jail guards at the Charlottetown jail had a certain amount of trust in William and did not make him wear leg irons during the day. In a last-ditch desperate attempt to flee from his problems, William took advantage of this and tried to escape custody. He stunned the guard by striking him on the head with a bottle, then shoved his way out of the cell. William sprinted for the jail courtyard but, when he couldn't find a way out of the secured yard, was quickly recaptured. Trust broken, William spent the last of his days in shackles.

William's fear of death continued until the moment he

died. He requested to be blindfolded before he left his cell — he didn't want to see the gallows. He wanted to see nothing of how the execution would happen.

On April 10, William was hanged in front of the Charlottetown jail. In the days leading up to his death, the *Daily Examiner* ran an editorial that implied that the practice of "courting at night," or unsupervised socializing, might be the cause of such a violent crime. The editorial encouraged parents to put a stop to the practice. Unfortunately for William Millman, such measures were too late.

Chapter 3
Hell at Sea

lexander Shaw was a lifelong seaman with a reputation for being a crusty, mean skipper. One former sailor described his service under Shaw as "hell on the sea." Shaw was known to "give a blow first and a curse later and was a born tyrant," the sailor said.

In October 1902, Shaw and the crew of the *Veronica* prepared to set off for South America from Mississippi. The ship was transporting a load of timber. Three crew members, Harry Flohr, Otto Monsson, and Fred Abrahamson, had served under Shaw and helped recruit other crewman for this voyage. Soon, Alexander MacLeod of Prince Edward Island was signed as the first officer, followed by Willem Smith, Alexander Bravo, Gustav Johansen, Julius Parsson, Gustav

Rau, Patrick Dorran, and Moses Thomas. The men were divided into two watches, with First Officer MacLeod teamed with Smith, Dorran, Johansen, and Flohr. Second Mate Abrahamson led Rau, Monsson, Parsson, and Bravo. Neither the captain nor cook, Moses Thomas, stood watch.

For the first few weeks, it was smooth sailing. Then Shaw mistakenly took them into the centre of the doldrums, the equatorial region of the Atlantic Ocean where waters are still and winds calm. Overshadowing the peacefulness was the constant threat of sudden, wicked storms and Shaw's frustration with trying to escape. With no sea current or breeze, the 56-metre *Veronica* could be stuck in the doldrums for a couple of weeks before it managed to catch a wind and break free.

There wasn't much for the crew to do while the ship sat idle. They talked about their lives at home and the families they left behind and gossiped about one another. Rau, Monsson, and Smith spent many hours together talking. Flohr, a German like Rau and Monsson, gravitated toward the group to talk of home.

It wasn't long before the 12 men aboard the *Veronica* began to grate on one another's nerves. Aggravation set in. Gossip turned vicious and animosity grew toward the first officer. MacLeod was a burly brute whom Captain Shaw had chosen specifically for his toughness. One evening, over a slight disagreement, MacLeod struck Smith. The man didn't fight back, but silently stewed about the punch, allowing the anger to fester.

As the hours turned into days, Rau, Monsson, Smith, and Flohr became increasingly bitter with the captain for landing them in the doldrums. Rations were cut back, and the four lamented over their hunger. Smith, still nursing his injury from MacLeod's punch, also talked about his growing hatred of the first officer. Feeding off one another's discontent, the four men developed a strong bond.

It's unclear how long the *Veronica* was stuck in the doldrums, but the discontent continued once she had resumed course — the crew's bitterness was eating away at them. Finally, Monsson and Rau decided they'd had enough. It was time for action. They told Flohr they were fed up with the captain and officers. They were going to kill the ship's officers and throw the bodies overboard. Rau told Flohr they had already decided he would help them. Despite their friendship, Flohr refused. The 19-year-old was frightened by the prospect of taking another man's life.

"I cannot murder or shoot any man," he told them.

Rau was infuriated. "Then you will let yourself be thrown overboard without resisting. It is all one to me whether you will or not," he said to Flohr.

With that, Flohr reluctantly agreed to become part of the scheme.

Smith was then brought into the conspiracy, and a few days later, Monsson, Smith, and Flohr gathered to hear Rau, the group's obvious leader, set out the plan's final details. He explained how the killings would take place and who would perform what job. Aside from being the mastermind of the finer points, Rau had also smuggled two revolvers on board, earning him instant respect from the group.

Rau figured that in order to kill the officers, a couple of others would also have to die, ensuring their actions remained secret. He instructed Smith and Flohr to kill Pat Dorran, who would be on lookout at the planned time. He would murder Julius Parsson himself. Parsson's bunk was located near the deck, and Rau didn't want to risk him over-hearing the scuffle.

Once these two men were dead, Rau told Smith and Flohr to meet him in the stern cabin, where Captain Shaw, First Officer MacLeod, Second Mate Abrahamson, and Moses Thomas slept. They would kill the four and throw their bodies into the sea. Monsson's job was to guard the other two crew members.

Around 2 a.m. on December 3, everything started out as planned. Smith began a casual conversation with Dorran, giving Flohr the opportunity to sneak up behind the man and slash his throat. But the conversation went on and on, and Flohr failed to appear.

Eventually running out of small talk, Smith, flaming mad, went looking for Flohr. He first found Rau, however, and told him of the failed plan. Flohr, it turned out, was simply too frightened to do the job. He was hiding below deck, waiting for the whole mess to be over.

When Rau found out that the first part of his plan had failed, he was furious. He knew that if the others couldn't do the job, he would have to do it himself. As Rau made his way toward the steps leading up to the deck, Flohr and Smith followed close behind.

On deck, Flohr, Smith, and Rau silently approached Dorran from behind. On his way, Rau picked up an iron belaying pin, a fastener used to secure rope. Standing with his hand behind his back, Rau asked Dorran to point out the North Star. The watchman crouched slightly to look under the mast, and Rau raised the pin in his hand, bringing it down on Dorran's head.

Dorran probably had no idea what hit him that first time, never mind the next two times. When Rau had finished, Dorran lay on the deck unconscious in a pool of blood, his face disfigured from the beating. Smith and Flohr dragged the limp man to an empty room. Flohr stood watch in the event Dorran regained his senses.

It must have been the sound of the man's body dropping that brought the first officer to the deck to have a look around. MacLeod called for Dorran when he noticed him missing from his post, then approached Rau and Smith and asked what was going on.

Once MacLeod was within reach, Rau struck again with the belaying pin. The man crumpled to the deck from the blow to his head. He lay in a heap, moaning in pain. Acting as though they were deaf to the sounds, Rau and Smith tossed the man overboard.

Rau then began to implement the second part of his plot. He attempted to rein Flohr further into the scheme, but the young man refused, arguing that Dorran needed continued guarding. Rau didn't take time to disagree as he and Smith resumed their path of destruction.

Moments later, Flohr heard two shots shatter the silence. Running to look through the door leading to the deck, he saw his friends come out of the second mate's room, each carrying a revolver. Abrahamson stumbled after them, crying out in pain and calling for the captain.

Throughout the mayhem, Julius Parsson was at the wheel, the result of an unexpected change in shifts. But then Rau gave the order that it was time for the man to die. Flohr, finally gathering his gumption, grabbed an iron belaying pin and headed toward his shipmate. Passing a pile of wooden fasteners, Flohr stopped to exchange the heavy iron pin for a lighter wooden one.

Parsson knew what was coming. He attempted to protect himself from the blows while keeping hold of the wheel. It was likely his fight for survival, combined with Flohr's feeble attempt at murder, that spared Parsson his life, for the moment.

Parsson took off running across the deck. He stopped short though when Rau arrived on the scene wielding his revolver. The man begged for his life and Rau, distracted by the captain at that moment, conceded. Parsson ran to hide.

Flohr had taken over the wheel, and Captain Shaw was making his way to the deck. As Shaw turned, he was startled by the sight of Rau, grasping an iron pin in one hand and a revolver in the other. There was no time for Shaw to think as Rau launched the pin through the air, followed quickly by two shots. The captain was hit, but not dead.

With his remaining strength, Shaw pushed past Rau and took cover below deck. He crawled into the navigation room, where Abrahamson had already sought refuge. The injured men blocked the door with tables and chairs. On the other side, Smith took up post to ensure they didn't escape.

Monsson had remained below deck throughout the ordeal, guarding Gustav Johansen and Alexander Bravo. Because they hadn't heard much from him for a while, Rau and Flohr decided to go check on him. They found Monsson standing in a puddle of blood under a port hole. Parsson had tried to escape, he told them, and he was forced to take action. He had struck the sailor with an iron pin and shoved him out the window.

"Look at this," Monsson said to Rau and Flohr. "It is a damn good belaying pin."

By this time, Patrick Dorran, the first man injured, had regained consciousness. He emerged from the holding room where he had been placed and begged for a glass of water. Rau responded, "All right. I'll give you a good drink. Harry, give me your belaying pin."

Flohr did as he was told, passing the tool to Rau. Then

he watched as the man again raised the heavy pin in the air and brought it down on his shipmate's skull. Dorran fell into a heap at Rau's feet. Again, Rau hardly seemed to notice the bloody remains. He ordered Flohr and Smith to get rid of the corpse, and Dorran was thrown overboard.

Of the 12 men who began the voyage on board the *Veronica*, 9 remained. The only men practically untouched by the horror were Alexander Bravo, Gustav Johansen, and Moses Thomas. Bravo and Johansen, under Monsson's guard, were likely just praying that their lives would be spared.

Thomas, however, was awake most of the night, startled from his sleep when Rau shot Abrahamson. Moving quietly and swiftly, the cook barricaded his door. He stayed still and silent, even as Rau raged outside his door, screaming, "If you don't come out, I'll break the door down and shoot you in your berth."

Whether Thomas was fiercely stubborn or frozen with fear, he stayed locked in his room all night. Rau eventually left, but returned in the morning, again fuming outside Thomas's door. Realizing Rau would eventually find a way in, the cook slowly opened the door. He was greeted by the sight of Rau, arm raised, clutching the revolver. Smith, standing nearby, interjected, "Don't kill him. He's done nothing to you."

The gang leader showed a moment of mercy and agreed. He searched the cook to make sure he was unarmed and, finding nothing, ordered Thomas to make breakfast.

As the meal cooked, Rau ordered the rest of the mutineers to secure the navigation room to make sure the captain and second mate were locked in tight. The men nailed wood planks across the doors and fastened ropes around the skylight, making sure the prisoners couldn't open the hatch.

However, Shaw and Abrahamson weren't in any shape to plan a great escape. They had both been shot twice. Each suffered neck wounds and shots to the stomach. In severe pain, the men were dying slow deaths inside their prison.

The gang extended the torture over several days. Shaw and Abrahamson were kept locked away with no food or water while the *Veronica* sailed aimlessly in the Atlantic Ocean near the equator. The men spent the time raiding the ship, rummaging through the belongings of their dead shipmates, and delving into the mail they were transporting, pocketing any valuables. Johansen and Bravo were smart enough to keep quiet and stay out of the way the whole time. A low profile might spare them from attack, they reasoned.

But Rau hadn't forgotten about them at all. He ordered Bravo and Johansen to join the rest of the crew and participate in the operation of the ship. Rau had finally decided they needed to get their act together and resume course. Unfortunately, the charts and instruments were locked in the navigation room with the captain and second mate. He needed that equipment if they were going to get back to sailing.

Armed with belaying pins and the two revolvers, the gang circled the skylight and stood ready as Rau untied the ropes securing the hatch. He yelled into the hole for the captain, but Abrahamson responded instead, emerging slowly onto the deck. Flohr, still being forced to take part, but seeing no other option, struck the second mate with an iron pin. Abrahamson was down, but still alive. Smith took his revolver and shot the man, striking him in the shoulder.

That was enough for Abrahamson. With the last of his strength, he threw himself overboard. Rau wasn't convinced the man would die, so as the second mate swam alongside the *Veronica*, the men shot into the water until his body disappeared in the ship's wake.

The gang returned their focus to the navigation room and the captain. Rau again called for the skipper to make an appearance.

Still Shaw didn't appear. Frustrated, Rau sent Bravo down with an axe to chase the captain out of hiding. Soon, Shaw came into sight, with Bravo close behind. He was barely able to walk, and his clothes were blood-soaked. The once shrewd and bad-tempered captain made a desperate plea for his life, begging for mercy.

"I will give you my gold watch. Please save my life. I have got a wife and children and I should like to see them again. If you will let me go, I will take you to any port you want," he implored.

Rau, showing a rare moment of empathy, ordered a crewman to bring the captain a drink.

The compassion was short-lived.

Shaw was told to come onto the deck. He staggered to the surface, shielding his head from the expected blow. Rau shoved a revolver at Flohr. The frightened young man shot at the captain three times, but yet again failed to make a fatal hit.

Rau once more took charge. He stepped up beside the captain, placed his revolver at the man's temple, and pulled the trigger. Bravo, Johansen, and the remaining crew threw the disfigured corpse into the ocean and the *Veronica* sailed on.

Almost half the crew, including all the officers, was now dead. Rau knew they couldn't remain at sea, hiding the bloodshed. He also knew that once they docked, questions would arise about the sparseness of the ship's crew. Realizing he needed a cover story, Rau came up with an elaborate and expansive tale that covered all the details. He required his crew to practise the script regularly.

This was their story: The *Veronica* ran into foul weather near Florida, and the main sail had been destroyed. While working on repairs high above deck, the first officer, MacLeod, had lost his footing and crashed to his death at his crewmates' feet.

Then yellow fever spread through the ship and claimed the second mate, Abrahamson, and two crewmen, all of whom had been buried at sea. Shortly afterward, a fire mysteriously erupted, and the crew was forced overboard into two lifeboats. One of the lifeboats overturned and all those on board perished. Only the remaining crew managed to survive. Rau was going to set the *Veronica* ablaze to support the tale.

The men were smart enough to know they would have to give the performance of a lifetime or else meet with Rau's fatal criticism. Unfortunately, Johansen and Bravo just couldn't nail down the story. During "rehearsals," they forgot lines, missed cues, and failed miserably at delivering a memorable performance.

Having no patience for the shoddy acting, Rau peppered Johansen with gunfire and shot Bravo in the head. Both men tumbled overboard.

As work to seal the details of the cover story continued, Moses Thomas baked bread and beans for provisions. A few days later, the five crewmen were ready to set off in the lifeboat. They piled clothing in a heap on the deck and doused it with lamp fuel. With the others waiting in the lifeboat, Rau struck a match and climbed into the boat. As they sailed away from the *Veronica*, they turned back to watch the ship erupt in flame. The next day, when they spotted land, they dumped their provisions into the ocean. They landed onshore and were discovered a few days later, on Christmas Day 1902, by a steamer ship, the *Brunswick*.

The cover story was played out for Captain George Brown of the *Brunswick* and apparently believed. But one night, Thomas decided he was finally going to take his fate into his own hands. He told Brown the true story. The captain, through some sixth sense, believed this story.

Rau also seemed to have a sixth sense and suspected the cook may have turned them in. He gathered the other men. They concocted a new tale, this time, placing the blame solely on Thomas. Later, when the men tried to pin everything on the cook, no one believed them.

The *Brunswick*, meanwhile, was making its way across the Atlantic Ocean, and Brown wasn't about to do anything to rock the boat. He said nothing of Thomas's story, treating Rau and his shipmates like guests. When the steamer docked in Liverpool, though, in mid-February, the police were waiting. Brown had sent word on ahead from an earlier stop.

Rau, Smith, Monsson, Flohr, and Thomas were taken into custody and questioned. Thomas's story to police remained unchanged from the tale he told Brown. His shipmates continued to be kept in the dark about his tale and stuck to their story that Thomas was the gang leader and instigator of the mutiny.

It didn't take long for that story to begin to unravel, though. After a few hours behind bars, separated from the rest of the gang, Flohr told police he wanted to make additional comments. He proceeded to reveal the same story as Thomas, fingering Rau as the head of the gang and mastermind of the plan.

With matching stories told by two men, the police and prosecuting lawyers decided to drop charges against Flohr and Thomas in exchange for their testimony. That left Gustav Rau, Willem Smith, and Otto Monsson charged with the murder of Alexander MacLeod, Julius Parsson, Patrick Dorran, Fred Abrahamson, Alexander Shaw, Gustav Johansen, and

Alexander Bravo. They were also charged with setting fire to the *Veronica*, conspiracy to murder, and piracy.

During the trial, Flohr and Thomas each lived up to their end of the bargain and told their accounts of the events on the *Veronica*. Their versions differed somewhat, with Thomas placing much of the blame on Flohr. However, Flohr stood his ground during his testimony, maintaining that Rau was behind the plan and the deaths.

Rau and Smith each took the stand to defend themselves, but Monsson stayed away from the witness stand. Rau made himself out to be intimidated by Flohr, saying he argued with everyone. As well, he expressed fear of Thomas, repeating that the cook was the mutiny's ringleader. The killings, Rau claimed, were planned and carried out by the others. He had no involvement. Smith echoed Rau's story, denying having a hand in the deaths. The closing statement, made by Monsson's lawyer, also gave credence to the cook masterminding the scheme.

The jury wasn't convinced. They quickly dismissed the idea that Thomas or Flohr was behind the plot and, 15 minutes after beginning deliberations, on May 14, 1903, returned with a guilty verdict for Rau, Smith, and Monsson. The men were sentenced to hang. However, the jury requested mercy for Monsson — they felt he had limited involvement in the mutiny. The judge agreed and granted clemency for the man.

Rau and Smith, on the other hand, bore full responsibility for creating their own hell at sea and died at the gallows.

Chapter 4
Desperate Measures

ay Bannister struggled to do the best she could for her family, but it was never enough. Never enough food, never enough money, never enough heat to keep them warm. Fed up, May was ready to do whatever she had to.

May and her four children, Daniel, Arthur, Frances, and Marie, lived in one of New Brunswick's most thickly wooded and bleak areas, about 10 kilometres from Moncton. In the grip of winter, their home was snowbound, accessible only by horse and sleigh or by foot along the railway track.

William Bannister, the children's father, had left the family around 1922. In the 13 years since, it had been a battle for survival. They moved often around southeast New Brunswick and Nova Scotia, always hoping for a better life. May and the older children did the best they could to provide for the family. Daniel and Arthur hunted, while May kept house for a widowed neighbour, Milton Trites, who ran a shoe store in Moncton. Milton had helped them build their home when they moved to the area.

Albert A. Powell and James Sargent were also kind to the family. Albert was from the Salvation Army and would bring groceries to the Bannisters. He then began to drop by Sunday mornings, teaching Bible lessons to May and the children. Before long, he was dropping by during the week and sometimes spending the night, sharing Daniel and Arthur's room.

Albert became a father figure in the home, especially to Frances. She sometimes asked him for money, and he always obliged with a few coins. He seemed genuinely concerned for the family's well-being. If he bumped into Frances and Marie in Moncton, he always made sure they had a way home, even if it meant hiring someone to get them there.

That's how James Sargent met the family. One night, Albert hired his friend James to drive the Bannister girls home. From then on, James, a baker, would often drop by the family's home with bread from his shop.

Despite May's income from her job with Milton and the food they received from Albert and James, May and her children still struggled to survive. Desperation finally drove May to devise a scheme that would bring her family out of its sense of desolation.

Her friendships with the three men would be the key.

It was no secret that Albert sometimes spent the night, but only the people inside knew that he bunked with Daniel and Arthur. It was also no secret that James was a frequent visitor, although he never spent the night. As well, May was known to occasionally spend the night at Milton's home.

May figured that if a new baby arrived in the home, she could blackmail each man with threats of publicly implicating him as the father. Facing this threat, the men would provide the Bannisters with an income to live on. She knew that it would be no trouble blackmailing Milton because they were in the midst of an affair. Her claim would be entirely possible, as far as Milton knew.

However, neither Albert nor James had made romantic advances toward May, so she knew her chances of becoming pregnant by either were slim. Regardless, it would still be easy to take advantage of their friendship. Albert had a keen interest in her daughters, so May decided that her youngest, 13-year-old Marie, could pretend to be carrying his baby. Careful not to sully her daughter's reputation too much, May accused only the one man of impregnating her daughter. As for James, she was prepared to become the mother of his fictional child.

Around the end of October 1935, the matriarch brought her children into the plan. She explained that they needed to find a baby. Daniel and Arthur, who regularly travelled the area hunting, knew of a family nearby who'd recently had a baby. Their mother drilled them for information, and Daniel and Arthur told her all they knew.

Philip Lake and his common-law wife, Bertha Ring, lived in a shack in Pacific Junction with their two children. John, also called Jackie, was young, they told their mother, but they weren't sure of his age. The boy was old enough to walk but not much older. The other child was a girl, Betty Ann, born only a few months earlier, they said. The Bannister boys had been out hunting and met Philip, who told them of the birth. The family was in obvious despair, worse off than the Bannisters themselves, the boys reasoned.

May couldn't have been happier. From what the boys told her, it was obvious the new baby was a burden to Philip. He and Bertha were probably wishing the child had never been born, she thought. For her purposes, the baby sounded like she was just the right age. May chose Arthur and Frances to go to the Lake home immediately and offer to take the child off their hands.

The siblings returned empty-handed. Philip had laughed at their request, even though the pair worked hard to convince him to let them have the baby. It was out of the question, he told them. He later told his friend Otto Blakeney that the outlandish request had bothered him. Knowing how much it would upset Bertha, he would keep it a secret from her.

May wasn't happy when her children arrived home without the baby. However, concerned they would run into difficulties, she had already started working on an alternate plan. If Philip and Bertha wouldn't give up their baby voluntarily, the Bannisters would have to be more forceful.

May began to lay the groundwork in the community. At the end of November, she quit her job with Milton and told him she was pregnant. He didn't ask about paternity, but she later volunteered that he was the father. Then, on Christmas Eve, May and Frances were shopping in Moncton, where May purchased a doll. Wrapping it carefully in a blanket, she opted to cuddle it close in her arms rather than carry the toy in a shopping bag. James drove them home and couldn't help but notice May cradling a baby during the trip.

On January 5, 1936, May decided it was time to take the plan to the next step. She made it perfectly clear to Daniel, Arthur, and Frances what needed to be done: go to the Lakes and bring home the baby. Do *whatever* needed to be done to get the child.

Late that evening, Arthur set off on the long walk alone, traipsing through the woods and sometimes walking along the railway tracks. It took nearly an hour to make the 10-kilometre hike to the Lake home.

Philip greeted the boy warmly, their past exchange over the child forgotten. He invited Arthur inside to warm up. A few hours later, in the early hours of January 6, Daniel and Frances arrived to help Arthur bring the new baby home.

When they reached the Lakes, Daniel and Frances knocked on the door and told Arthur they had arrived. They remained outside as Arthur closed the door, going back in. Moments later, he reopened the door and handed the infant to his sister. With babe in arms, she and Daniel left, heading toward the railway tracks and straight for home.

Only once did Frances look back, glimpsing the orange glow of fire in the January night sky. She continued to plod through the snow, carrying the infant girl wrapped in a blanket, even when she heard a woman scream for help and her footsteps behind her, even when she heard what sounded like a shot come from inside the house.

As Frances and Daniel made their way, Arthur caught up with them. They arrived home around 2:30 a.m., raising their mother from bed. She happily took the baby and nestled the new arrival into her own bed.

Later that day, Otto Blakeney was more than ready for lunch when he took a break from chopping wood. Despite the cool temperature, he had worked up a sweat. He made his way along the deep, snowy path toward Philip Lake's house. A few days earlier, Philip had invited him for dinner, knowing his bachelor friend would be working hard splitting wood.

Otto had readily accepted the invitation and was looking forward to the visit. Bertha made a good meal, and Philip was always cheerful and laid-back. He had an easy smile that showed off two gold teeth, giving him a memorable grin. The two had become fast friends last spring, when they'd bumped into each other at the train station. For a while, Otto had camped in Philip's backyard and had even helped take care of the couple's young boy in the fall, when Bertha left to have their other child.

Walking out of the woods and into the clearing, Otto was shocked to find the Lake home reduced to a smouldering pile of ashes. Frantically searching for Philip, Otto found charred remains among the cinders, but he refused to believe it was his friend. There was no sign of Bertha or their two children.

Otto quickly set out for the home of Omar Lutes, the nearest neighbour, hoping Philip and the rest of the family had rushed there for help. Along the way, he made another grim discovery when he found a baby bottle, full of frozen milk, at the edge of the woods. A few more steps revealed a large patch of blood in the snow. Soon, he stumbled across Bertha's half-naked body frozen in the snow, a severe gash on her head. Nearby, the body of young John also lay frozen. As he continued his search for help, Otto anxiously wondered what had happened to Philip and Betty Ann. Perhaps the father and daughter had managed to escape.

The Lutes home was empty, so Otto rushed to the nearby train station, where Omar worked. Finding the neighbour at his job, Otto recounted his grisly discovery and explained that Philip and the baby were missing. Omar notified Moncton police and the RCMP, and the two men returned to the Lake home, hoping to find Philip and the baby.

Carefully looking over the ruins of the home, Otto and Omar soon figured out their friend's fate. Lying in the ashes was a skull with gold teeth. As they tried to come to grips with the tragedy, police arrived and began their investigation.

Over the next several days, police searched the scene.

Investigators quickly concluded that Philip, Bertha, their 20-month-old son, John, and 6-month-old daughter, Betty Ann, appeared to have been murdered. They also conceded that their tiny home had likely burned down quickly. Built mostly out of junk boards from the Canadian National Railway, it was covered in tar paper outside and paste board and old newspapers inside. The blaze's intensity was apparent with the family alarm clock. A dollop of molten glass had dripped onto the hands of the still-ticking clock, freezing time at 11:15.

Examining the yard, police found several sets of footprints in the freshly fallen snow. While some were Omar's and Otto's, there were others. Police followed them to Bertha's body, along a path to the railway tracks, and on to the Bannister home. On the way, they found a blue and white striped mitten tucked inside a leather mitten.

Knocking on the door of the Bannisters' small two-storey home in Barry Mills, police were greeted by Daniel. The young man acknowledged the mitten was his but explained that he'd loaned the pair to his brother, Arthur, a few days ago. That, along with an eyewitness who identified Arthur walking along the railway tracks the night of the fire at the Lake home, was enough for police to take him into custody.

On January 7, the 18-year-old clean-cut young man with long blond hair and gentle blue eyes was charged with murdering Philip Lake. Daniel, 21, was arrested the next day and also charged with murder. At the same time, 15-year-old Frances was taken into custody as a material witness.

Police said that all three Bannisters were at Philip Lake's home when a fight started, the fire erupted, and Lake and his family met their demise. Frances was up front answering police questions, spelling out most of the details. One detail she left out, though, was that their mother had cooked up the whole scheme.

Police made several trips to the Bannisters as they continued to gather details about the crimes. They had nagging doubts about the infant — they suspected her tiny body had been cremated in the inferno, but weren't totally convinced. They were also curious about the baby at the Bannister home, discovered when they went to collect evidence against Arthur and Daniel.

Police noticed that the child's hair was burned on one side and the other side had just been cut. When they suggested the child might be the missing Lake baby, May flatly denied the accusation. The child was her own, she insisted. Still, police asked more questions, and May became indignant.

During one trip police made to the home to specifically talk about the baby, May refused to let them see her. When they asked to look through the home for the child, she objected. Since they had no search warrant, all they could do was stand at the door.

May, however, did answer some of their probing questions. She claimed she gave birth to the child at a cabin in nearby Fox Creek, but couldn't remember the cabin's exact location. She said a French woman had assisted with the birth, but couldn't recall her name. The child was born a few months ago, she said. This claim contradicted what a neighbour had already told police — he'd never seen the infant at the home until the Monday just past, in the hours following the fire at the Lakes'.

May's story didn't convince police. The day after Daniel was charged with murder, she was taken into custody as a material witness. Police took the baby to the Moncton Hospital, where she was hungry but otherwise in good health. On January 10, police charged a furious May Bannister with kidnapping. She was the first person in New Brunswick to face this charge.

With so many of the Bannisters in custody, the Moncton City Police Station was packed. Frances, who was always cheerful, lounged away the hours in the women's section. Arthur, instead of being kept with the harder, older criminals, was placed in the juvenile ward and watched closely by guards. Daniel was kept in the regular lock-up with the other inmates. Their mother took up residence in the station's waiting room, because she needed the extra space for Marie, who had no place else to go. In the lobby, police screened off an area and set up a bed, table, and chairs. A matron kept close watch over the mother and her youngest child.

Since the news of the fire at Pacific Junction broke, community interest in the case was high. The *Moncton Transcript* ran detailed accounts of the investigation. Like the police, Monctonians were trying to figure out why May Bannister would kidnap the infant girl and what role Arthur, Daniel, and Frances had played in the escapade.

When the entire family, except Marie, appeared before the judge on January 13 to face their various charges, thousands of spectators turned out in downtown Moncton. They began filtering into the courtroom hours ahead of the scheduled court appearances and kept coming until about 300 were packed into the seats. Hundreds more hung around on Duke Street outside the court and near the police station. The crowd caused such a disruption the street was closed to traffic.

Arthur and Daniel were charged with the murder of Philip Lake and Bertha Ring. In addition, they were charged with the abduction of the couple's daughter, Betty Ann Lake. May was charged with kidnapping and every angle of the charge, including forcibly seizing the infant, procuring and counselling her sons and daughter to forcibly seize the baby, "taking away" the little girl in order to deprive her mother of her possession, and assisting her children in the abduction of the child by harbouring her. Frances never faced charges, yet she remained in jail as a material witness and was held on $10,000 bail, until after the trial of her brothers and mother.

Each preliminary hearing was held in Moncton, but when the cases went before the jury, the venue was changed to district court in Dorchester, 34 kilometres away, before Chief Justice Jeremiah Hayes. Community interest remained high. Hotel rooms were booked, and trains from Moncton were packed as curious onlookers made the trip to hear the details.

During the court proceedings, Arthur was always neatly dressed, looking innocent and wide-eyed. Daniel presented a different image and was described in local newspapers as "unkept and dirty." His sandy-coloured hair was uncombed, his clothing worn and rumpled. Daniel's appearance reflected his family's poverty — he was described as looking "undernourished." He also appeared bewildered at what was going on. Police had to guide him to his seat in the prisoner's dock.

Arthur was first to stand trial, then May faced her kidnapping charges. Daniel was the last to be tried. During the trials, it became evident there was confusion over how Bertha was actually dealt her fatal blow. A coroner's jury had already concluded that she had died of a fractured skull, an injury that completely destroyed a portion of her brain. The autopsy also revealed that she was three months' pregnant.

One theory suggested she'd got in the middle of a scuffle between Arthur and her husband while the men were drinking. After being struck, she staggered out in search of help, when she eventually collapsed and died in the snow. But doctors who conducted the autopsy contradicted that account, stating she wouldn't have been able to move after suffering such a severe blow. Another report suggested she was hit after walking in on a fight between the men and that Arthur took her with him when he escaped the flames.

There was uncertainty as well over Philip Lake's final

moments, and neither Arthur's nor Daniel's trials cleared up the confusion. Philip's remains were badly charred, with most of the skin burned off. A large skull fracture revealed some of his brain tissue, and the doctor who performed the autopsy claimed that his organs had been cooked during the blaze. He did discover a bullet in Philip's head, although he was unable to determine if the bullet had been the cause of death.

Frances turned out to be the star witness of the trials when she provided the missing link between her family and the reason behind the kidnapping and deaths. Police still hadn't figured out that May was the mastermind behind the ploy. The picture started to become clear, though, after Frances readily testified that she and her brothers were carrying out their mother's instructions.

Then Milton, Albert, and James testified, casting even more light on May's role. Each took the stand and told of May's accusations of fathering the new baby. She didn't come right out and say it, they testified, but May strongly alluded to the possibility of blackmail unless they started paying her money to support the child. All told her to forget it.

With this evidence, the extent of the Bannisters' poverty and desperation was revealed. It was no secret the family was poor, but after the jury heard the damning testimony of the three friends, it was obvious the family would do anything to survive.

Arthur, Daniel, and May Bannister were each found

guilty of the charges they faced.

Arthur and Daniel paid the ultimate price for their part in the plan, created and orchestrated by their mother. The brothers were hanged on September 23, 1936, accompanied by Frances and Marie. Their long-lost father, William, who had walked away from his family more than a decade ago, was also in attendance at their death.

The only one missing was the family matriarch. She was incarcerated at Kingston Penitentiary in Ontario, sentenced to a three-and-a-half–year term for kidnapping. Because of May, five people, including her own sons, were dead. Regardless, she earned an early release for good behaviour.

Chapter 5
Spellbound

t must have been an incredible atmosphere. A handful of English-speaking new immigrants in a small, rural, largely Francophone community in southeastern New Brunswick, gripped by religious fervour. So great was their frenzy, the group met for hours on end in early 1805. When not worshipping together, they walked about in a trancelike state, as if under a spell.

It all started a year earlier, when siblings Amasa and Jonathan Babcock were new to Shediac Bridge. The brothers farmed, fished, worked in the woods, and lived an uncomplicated life. History remembers them as "hard-working settlers of slight education" who were "easily moved to go to extremes on occasions of excitement." Amasa was married with nine children. The men's sister, Mercy, also lived with Amasa.

Although from a Baptist background, the Babcock family occasionally went to Sunday service at the house of William Hanington. The first English-speaking resident in the area, William had settled into a place of prominence in the 20 years he'd been there and was a leader among the English. On Sundays, a small gathering met at his home to hear him read from the Church of England service book.

Perhaps the conservative Church of England services weren't lively enough for the Babcocks and other Baptists in the area, or maybe they were searching for messages and beliefs more closely linked to what they had practised at home in England. But in the spring of 1804, the few Baptist families of the area began to hold revival meetings at the Babcock home. They started slow, meeting every Sunday night. But their thirst grew and it wasn't long before they were meeting Thursday evenings, too. Eventually, they outgrew the Babcock home and moved to a hall. The group was so intensely focused on its religion that some even believed the world was ending.

The group welcomed visitors, both worshippers and preachers. A Moncton preacher attended a meeting, holding a more traditional Baptist service. Two travelling evangelists stopped in for a few days, sharing their message.

Then along came Jacob Peck.

There is no record of his religious background, but Jacob was known to travel, spreading his spiritual fervour. He seemed to have a charisma that captured worshippers and whipped them into frenzy. Especially vulnerable were the innocent or poorly educated, such as those he found around Shediac Bridge.

During Jacob's religious meetings, followers would fall into trances, appear to be possessed, and utter incomprehensible messages from their dazed state. One of his meetings in Shediac Bridge went throughout the night, and worshippers experienced "the most extraordinary scenes of religious excitement," historians say.

At another revival meeting that went well into the night, Amasa Babcock's daughter Sarah and another local girl, Sarah Cornwall, apparently fell into a trance. The Babcock girl began to talk of the impending end of the world. So enraptured was the congregation, they wanted these prophecies recorded, but since none of them was able to read or write, William Hanington was sent for to note the special event.

William dismissed the request for secretarial duties, but the Baptists persisted. Hoping to capture at least a portion of a night's sleep, and thinking he might convince them of their foolishness, William relented and made his way to the revival. By now, both girls were muttering how they would change the French Catholic settlers to Baptist and how William himself would convert to their religion.

William was unable to convince the Baptists that the girls were talking nonsense. Instead, the predictions stirred the congregation's religious zeal and gave them fodder for future gatherings. Early in 1805, one revival meeting went day and night for a week. Amasa and his family "appear to have been wholly out of their minds," state accounts of the event. Jacob, seeing the mania he helped create, apparently decided it was time to move on and left Shediac Bridge.

In February, a few days after Jacob's departure, Amasa and Jonathan Babcock returned to Amasa's farm after another revival meeting. Inside the farmhouse, the siblings milled some grain, then Amasa proceeded to dust the flour onto the floor. "This is the bread of heaven," he whispered as the flour fell. His wife later said that he then removed his shoes and socks and rushed into the icy cold winter night, shouting, "The world is to end! The world is to end! The stars are falling!"

Returning to the kitchen, Amasa lined up his family along a bench, in order from oldest to youngest. He began to sharpen a folding knife, then approached Mercy and ordered her to remove her dress, get on her knees, and prepare for death. Without apparently a second thought, Mercy did as she was told. She had been attending the revivals with the rest of the family and was just as spellbound.

Amasa then approached Jonathan and told him to remove his clothes. The brother obeyed and watched as Amasa drove the knife into their sister "with savage strength." Within seconds, she was dead.

The sight of blood seemed to awaken some of the Babcock family from their trance. Jonathan, still naked, bolted into the night and ran about a half kilometre to the nearest neighbour. Once he was dressed, he and the neighbour rushed to William's.

Because of his prominence among the English, William was the obvious person to go to for help. However, with no official power, he momentarily considered staying out of the whole affair. But he quickly reconsidered — Amasa Babcock wasn't in any state of mind to be wandering around free, William decided. At the same time, he made another decision: he wasn't going after Amasa by himself. He set off toward Joseph Poirier Sr.'s house to enlist the help of his sons.

William was delayed briefly when he lost his way and ended up at the wrong house. Redirected, he found the muscle he sought. It was about 2 a.m. when William and two of Poirier's sons made their way to Amasa's house.

When the men arrived, Amasa was calmly strolling about the kitchen, the rest of his family sitting bewildered on the bench. William instructed the Poirier boys to seize the accused murderer, but Amasa fought back. He demanded to know what they were going to do. When William told him he was going to be held for the murder of Mercy, Amasa yelled to his two sons "Gideon's men, arise." The sons joined in the wrestling and tried to defend their father, but the Poiriers gained the upper hand. Seizing Amasa's hands behind his back, they secured them with a rope.

Once Amasa was restrained, William looked around the Babcock home but saw no sign of Mercy's body. Amasa refused to say what he had done with the corpse. His wife and children also remained silent. Amasa's wife would only acknowledge that the woman was dead. The men took Amasa to William's house for the remainder of the night.

With Amasa removed from the situation, the family opened up, saying that Amasa had taken his sister's remains outside after Jonathan left. It's unclear whether Amasa was still gripped in his religious stupor, but after dumping the body, he walked home backward, sweeping his footprints from the snow as he retreated.

Reason seemed to come and go for Amasa over the next few hours. The attempt to hide his tracks may have been a sign of sanity, but the moment was short-lived. As the Poiriers and William led him away, he had triumphantly yelled "Aha! Aha! It was permitted!" apparently making a reference to a Bible passage.

News of Mercy's slaying quickly spread among the community. By sunrise, all of the area's English-speaking residents began a search for the body. At the same time, Mercy's death and Amasa's apparently insane actions seemed to jolt the entranced Baptist community out of its religious spell. When Mercy's body was found, disembowelled in a snowbank, it was another shake back to reality.

At daylight, William and the Poirier brothers set off with Amasa for their walk to Dorchester, about 40 kilometres away, to deliver Amasa to the nearest jail. But when the prisoner flew into another religious fit, they had to stop at another Baptist's house. There, Amasa became so violent and senseless, his arms had to be restrained as he was tied to a bed.

While the group was stopped, a snowstorm settled in, and it was another three days before they could continue. When the weather cleared, Amasa's arms were tied together and he was placed in a one-horse sled. Wearing snowshoes, William and the Poirier brothers took turns pulling Amasa through the woods.

The rest of the trip was uneventful and upon their arrival, Amasa was promptly charged with murder. It wasn't until June, though, that the case went to trial. The trial lasted just six hours. The jury took only about 30 minutes to decide that Amasa was guilty of killing his sister. Sentenced to die, he was hanged on February 28, 1806, and buried in Dorchester.

When he heard of Amasa's pending trial, Jacob Peck wandered back to the area to provide moral support — and likely satisfy his curiosity about what happened the night Mercy was killed. To his surprise though, he was also charged in the same court, on the same day that Amasa's trial started.

The presiding judge saw Jacob as being ultimately responsible for throwing Amasa, and much of the rest of the community, into the spiritual whirl that resulted in Mercy's death. He charged Jacob with "blasphemous, profane and seditious language at the (revival) meetings."

Having money at hand, Jacob paid bail and left prison. When his court date rolled around and he was to answer for the "very frantic, irregular and even impious manner" in which he held his revival meetings, he never showed up. Jacob Peck seems to have disappeared from the pages of history.

Chapter 6
A Deadly Visit Home

n March 19, 1791, Nicholas Eisenhaur awoke around 4 a.m. to see an orange light flickering across the ceiling and walls of his home. He rose from the warm covers of his bed and went to the window, peering out. Across the water, the home of his good friend George Frederick Eminaud was engulfed in flames.

Nicholas sent his son for their friend Joseph Contoy. Although neighbours, Joseph and Nicholas lived some distance apart, each on his own peninsula. Both were separated from the inferno at the Eminaud home by the frigid waters of Mahone Bay, in the Lunenburg area of Nova Scotia.

The fastest way to George's house was across the bay on ice floes that were just starting to break up after a long winter. Nicholas, Joseph, and their sons left from Nicholas's house for the treacherous trip. Jumping from one piece of ice to another as fast as possible, they watched helplessly as flames consumed the home. By the time they arrived, little was left standing except the chimney. Another neighbour arrived about the same time, and Joseph sent him for George's son Frederick, who lived close by.

Although darkness still surrounded the scene, by the glow of the embers, Joseph could just make out what appeared to be a body among the ashes, lying along a floor beam. Using a garden hoe found in the shed, the group managed to drag the remains within reach, where they could examine them more closely.

It was a ghastly find. The limbs had been burned off, and Joseph later said the insides had been consumed by fire. Where the torso's back had rested on the floor beam, parts of skin were still intact, although burnt and shrivelled "like parchment," Joseph said. The charred corpse was unrecognizable.

The clothing confirmed the men's worst suspicions, though. The remains were George's. Bits of his well-known jacket and a red shirt were still intact, as well as pieces of woollen clothes he used to wear underneath because of his rheumatism. George's signature handkerchief was still tied around his neck.

The remains were found near where George's bed would have sat. The group of friends acknowledged that even though the man was known to go to bed around 9 p.m., he never slept in his clothes. In addition, they had found blood on his clothes, between the shoulders. This left little doubt that something had gone seriously wrong at the house earlier in the night.

Adding to the dreadful feeling was the absence of George's wife and granddaughter. Later, as night turned to day, the men discovered bones "here and there" throughout the ruins, the only evidence of the woman's and child's bodies.

At daybreak, about 6 a.m., the men began to look around the yard, searching for clues that would help them figure out what had happened. George's hat was found about three metres from the front door of the house, covered in blood and partially buried in snow. Another large patch of blood coloured the snow about half a metre away.

Two sets of footprints were obvious in the heavy, wet spring snow. They traipsed around the house's cinders and into the woods behind George's house. Although several men from the area had gathered at the home by this time, none of them had travelled to or from the woods.

Later in the day, George Bohner, a local guide, was brought in to track the footsteps. Bohner traced the path through the woods and down to the ice floes, picking up the trail on the other shore. Eventually, the footsteps led to the woods, where a flat-bottomed boat had been stashed and then obviously launched into the bay.

Many footprints lined the banks of Mahone Bay, but the prints Bohner followed were made by two men wearing moccasins, fairly uncommon footwear for the area. The tracks also led to barren and isolated areas, Bohner pointed out to the men at the scene of the fire. Piecing the clues together, the men concluded that the culprits were visiting town and had been hiding in the woods near George's house, waiting for their chance to attack.

Hiking through desolate woods was second nature for John James Boutilier, 26, and his 22-year-old brother, George Frederick. The men had grown up in Lunenburg but now lived in Tatamagouche. Although it was on the other side of the province, the brothers often returned home to visit their mother, 10 siblings, and other relatives and friends.

The trek from Tatamagouche to Lunenburg was a hard one. Even in summer, it took several days. But in March, the woods would still have been snowed in and the ice just starting to break up in the bays around the province. The going would not be easy. That didn't deter the brothers — they were anxious to visit their hometown. They packed a few belongings in backpacks and left home on March 7.

After a nine-day journey, the men arrived at their mother's home on March 16. She was glad to see her boys after their long winter's absence and was reluctant to let them go. When they mentioned wanting to visit their uncle, she chided them, telling her boys that if their uncle wanted to see them, he could come to them — she wanted to spend as much time as possible with her sons before they returned to Tatamagouche. John and George Frederick agreed to stay put, barely poking their noses out the door during the visit.

The Boutilier brothers spent two days in Lunenburg before setting off on March 18. Their first stop was their 24-year-old brother David's schooner in Indian Point. After a brief visit of only a few hours, John and George Frederick continued on their way home to Tatamagouche.

It wasn't long before the community started to talk about the unusual spring visit by the Boutilier brothers. The more residents talked about the deaths of the Eminauds and their granddaughter and the brothers' visit, the more suspicion against them grew. Some even spoke of seeing the brothers near the Eminaud home prior to the blaze.

From the onset of the investigation, police considered John and George Frederick prime suspects. However, the sheriff didn't catch up with the pair until they reached Halifax on March 24. They denied visiting the Eminauds this time around. They admitted that they knew George, but hadn't been to his house in about four years. As the probe continued, police rifled through the brothers' belongings and found enough vital evidence to officially accuse them of murder.

The brothers were charged with "not having the fear of God before their eyes, but being moved and seduced by the instigation of the Devil" and planning the assault of George Frederick Eminaud. The charge accused them of using "certain large sticks of no value" and said they struck and beat

George and inflicted "several mortal strokes, wounds and bruises." George Frederick was also accused of striking the victim on the head with a tomahawk and killing him instantly. John faced an additional charge of "aiding, helping, abetting, assisting, comforting and maintaining" George Frederick with the fatal blow.

The trial started May 4. Over the next several days, the men maintained their innocence, even as their own siblings cast doubt on their story. John Peter, the youngest of the Boutilier siblings, recounted how one night, as the three men were talking during their visit, John and George Frederick mentioned staying at "old Eminaud's" before arriving at their mother's.

Brother David told a different story than his brothers when it came to their visit to Indian Point. John and George Frederick maintained they had arrived at 9 p.m. the evening of March 18. However, David said they didn't arrive until the next morning, only hours before sunrise — not long after the Eminauds' house was discovered in flames.

But one seemingly insignificant object sealed their fate.

When the Boutilier brothers had been arrested and authorities rifled through their possessions, they examined the snowshoes, moccasins, a tomahawk — and a broken piece of chalk.

The day before his death, George and his son Frederick had been working on a construction project. George had broken a piece of chalk in half, keeping a portion for himself and giving the other bit to his son. During the trial, Frederick produced his piece of chalk, an exact fit to the piece found in possession of the Boutilier brothers.

After hearing the evidence, the jury quickly reached a guilty verdict for both men. They were sentenced to hang the next day, May 9, in what the judge said must be an example to other would-be killers.

Although a verdict had been reached and the sentence rendered, there were still many mysteries about the case. But just before John and George Frederick Boutilier made their way to the gallows, many unanswered questions were resolved. As was tradition, a priest was present with the men just before the hanging. At the eleventh hour, they admitted their guilt and filled in the missing details.

Following the execution, the priest wrote the chief justice. "At last, after long exhortation, the stony hearts became mollified, and, in a flood of tears, they owned themselves guilty." He then recounted their confessions about what really happened that fatal night.

The brothers had been having a tough go of it in Tatamagouche. They needed money and knew George Eminaud probably had some stashed away. He'd openly talked about his money on previous visits, and it was common knowledge around Lunenburg that he kept money in his house.

With the sole purpose of killing George and taking his money on the night of March 15, the brothers travelled across the province. But upon their arrival, they changed their minds, saying only that God had prevented them. So they stayed in the community at their mother's home until March 18.

That evening, the men knocked on George's door and asked him if they could spend the night. The elderly man agreed, gladly welcoming them in. George knew they needed someplace soft to sleep and went to the barn to get fresh straw for their beds. George Frederick and John followed him right out.

The brothers then attacked George with sticks they found near the door. The priest recounted, "He made little resistance and ... both of them gave him repeated blows." Despite the vicious beating, the brothers told the priest they didn't think George was bleeding. They left his crumpled body in the snow and went back into the house, killing his wife and granddaughter the same way.

After the beatings, John and George Frederick broke into George's chest to take the money they'd come for. While staying with their mother, they'd heard that George was expecting repayment on a £50 loan (about $9,500 today). But they were sorely disappointed — inside was only £10. Angry, frustrated, and high on adrenaline, the brothers ransacked the house, taking whatever else they could find. They searched George's body, pocketing the piece of chalk without even thinking about it.

Once they had scoured the house, John and George

Frederick knew they had to leave quickly. They piled the three bodies together in the centre of the kitchen. In a final show of disrespect, they covered the bodies with the same straw George had gathered for their beds. Before walking out the door, the Boutilier brothers took a burning ember from the stove and touched it to the straw. They told the priest that they did not know the house had burned to the ground until they reached Halifax.

The brothers said they had maintained their innocence because they believed they would be exonerated. With no witnesses, they were convinced the evidence would never lead back to them. However, they acknowledged the justness of the sentence, confessing they had no wish to live. They appeared truly remorseful, especially George Frederick, the priest stated. In fact, their apologetic demeanour impressed the priest, who concluded, "The behaviour of both of them was such that, had they not been murderers, they might have been called Christian heroes."

Chapter 7
Poor Charlotte

**S**tumbling across the small fire was purely an accident. Had the weather been poor or the season's growing conditions not just right, Isaiah Munro would have waited for another day to harvest his hay crop. But in late August 1880, it was shaping up to be a fine day to cut hay.

Isaiah had gathered several of his brothers to help. Just as they were about to start working, they noticed a plume of smoke rising from one of their fields. They were in a remote part of Nova Scotia's Annapolis Royal. No one was in sight, and they were surprised that someone had left a fire smouldering, especially so close to their ripe, dry hay. Knowing how fast a fire could spread, Isaiah and his brothers rushed to extinguish the embers.

As he approached the smouldering brush, Isaiah became distinctly aware of two unusual things: he could smell meat burning, and a fire was still burning under some rocks. He also noticed something much more disturbing: "Before I got there I saw a bone sticking through the rocks ... and a foot sticking out," he recalled later.

There was no mistaking — it was a human foot.

The brothers sent for the coroner, about 16 kilometres away. Dr. Bingay later described the grisly scene. The victim was a woman and her body was badly burned. Her legs were completely consumed by the flames, but her upper body and face were still recognizable. The woman was found lying on her back, the skin on her arms shrivelled from the heat, her right hand burned off at the wrist. Bingay estimated that she was about six months' pregnant and said she was alive when set on fire. After Bingay's examination, a police photographer took some pictures and the remains were placed in a box and taken to police.

In the small community, the woman was soon identified as Charlotte Hill. Her friend Addie Scott had agreed to the grim task of identifying the remains. It was common knowledge the women were residents of one of the local poorhouses, the government's cheap way of looking after those unable to support themselves. Addie also confirmed that Charlotte hadn't been seen for a couple of days.

Charlotte Hill was one of about eight illegitimate children of a woman named Mary Purdy and began living in poorhouses when she was a child. The toil of her hard life had left her with withered features, rounded shoulders, and many front teeth missing, making her look older than the 30-something she was. Friends knew she was a deeply unhappy woman who had threatened to take her own life in the past. She was also known to regularly run away from the poorhouse and the care of its keeper, Joseph Thibault.

Joseph Thibault was a pillar of the community, a man in a position of great trust. At 45, he was known as a skilled businessman and successful farmer. Historians say he was also an expert cattle trader. In addition to his business interests, Joseph was the keeper of the poorhouse in the Nova Scotia community of North Range, just south of Digby.

Once Charlotte's identity was confirmed, it didn't take much to link her to Joseph. Both Charlotte and Joseph weren't at the house on August 31, some of the other residents stated, but Joseph returned alone the next day. Others told of seeing Joseph and a woman travelling in the early morning hours of September 1, but seeing him awhile later, alone.

On September 3, three days after Charlotte's body was found, the poorhouse keeper was taken into custody at his family's home. The two constables sent to make the arrest found him sitting at his kitchen table, his head resting in his hands. His young daughter sat beside him. Joseph was calm and did not resist arrest, although he proclaimed his innocence.

"I was looking for you, but I am not the right man," he

told the officers. As other investigators searched the residence and property for evidence, Joseph was taken to court to be charged.

An angry mob was waiting for him. News of the murder and the vile conditions of Charlotte's body had spread quickly. Residents were disgusted by the crime's brutality. Once Joseph was implicated in the death, they were outraged that such a trusted citizen could be capable of the crime. In the minds of many, he was guilty before he was even formally charged.

Tension was high when the handcuffed man arrived at the courthouse. Officers guarding him knew the crowd was anxious — calls of "Take him out" and "Hang him" rose above the din. When someone in the throng yelled, "Are you guilty of this crime?" Joseph hollered back, "I don't know anything about a crime, people say I am."

Once inside, the crowd dispersed and Joseph was charged with the murder of Charlotte Hill. He pleaded not guilty.

As the investigation continued, public interest in the case remained high. Citizens were anxious to see justice done. The trial began on December 1. As it unfolded, it turned into a spectacular event. The excitement over hearing the details of Charlotte's atrocious death created a morbid anticipation in the courtroom.

The curiosity spilled into the rest of Nova Scotia and into New Brunswick. Newspaper reporters flooded Annapolis Royal, sending detailed stories back to their offices by telegraph. Accounts of the trial were carried in the *Weekly*

Monitor, the local *Weekly Journal*, the *Halifax Chronicle*, and the *Saint John News*.

By the trial's final day, December 6, the interest had reached a fever pitch. "This morning the court room was packed, people being literally piled on top of each other in some places," reported the *Chronicle*. "The court room was packed all day, the audience bringing lunches in their pockets ... People have come from all over Annapolis, King's, Digby, Queen's and Hants Counties, and even from Saint John ... all the hotels tonight are crowded to their utmost capacity."

The intense interest by the press didn't go unnoticed by court officials. Defence lawyer Robert Motton urged the jury to disregard anything they may have read. The prosecuting lawyers, however, revelled in the public scrutiny. The drama and brutality of Charlotte's death, along with the growing hostility toward the accused, let them paint Joseph as a villain. In his opening address, a prosecutor wondered whether "the fiendish author of the crime stood by and gloated over her agony" as Charlotte was consumed by flames.

Joseph's appearance didn't help his case. After three months in jail, gone was his heavy-set frame, dark complexion, and "very calm" demeanour, described the *Monitor*. Reports noted his pale complexion, loss of weight, and overall conduct. "He sits in a crouching attitude, his keen dark eyes riveted on the faces of the witnesses, but displays no emotion," the *Monitor* reported.

As witnesses told their stories about Charlotte Hill and

Joseph Thibault, a series of circumstances, all with Joseph at the centre, unfolded. The *Monitor* reported that "link after link is brought out in the chain of evidence" against Joseph, each putting the poorhouse keeper in the wrong place at the wrong time.

Some residents told of seeing Thibault early one morning in the late summer, travelling with a woman. They recalled how quickly he was driving the horse and wagon, despite the road's poor condition.

"[I] had known Thibault very well," testified Thomas Berry. "There was a woman with him. Thibault was driving very fast ... I have always stopped to talk with him when I met him. He did not stop on this occasion ... He drove pretty fast for a rough road."

William Router testified that he also saw Joseph and a woman early one morning in the late summer. Later, they met again. "There was a man and woman passed, going east," Router stated, adding, "Shortly after this the same man passed me ... it may have been about two hours or two and a half after he passed us ... He was alone and in his shirt sleeves. He was driving pretty smart."

Charlotte's friend Addie Scott testified that the last time she saw Charlotte, she was packing, putting her few possessions in a basket. Charlotte had told Addie she was running away.

When Herbert Rhoddy took the stand, he told of taking a load of lumber through the back roads near the Munros' land. Armed with his rifle in case he had the chance to do some hunting, Rhoddy said he stopped his wagon when a partridge flew across the road and into the woods. He followed the bird, gun in hand, to a swamp, where he discovered a basket filled with women's clothing.

Frank Barrett, a police officer, talked of discovering Joseph's wagon hidden in the woods about 260 metres from Joseph's barn. The wagon had been covered with spruce trees and bushes. Barrett had seized the wagon and brought it to the courthouse yard as evidence.

One of the last witnesses to take the stand against the accused was Ann Thibault, Joseph's wife. Moments after she was sworn in, her husband's lawyer stood to remind her that because she was married to the defendant, she was not required to answer any questions. That seemed to suit her just fine. Ann spoke not a word while in the witness stand.

When giving his closing summation, Joseph's lawyer said the prosecution was trying to make it appear as though Joseph had committed the murder in an attempt to cover up Charlotte's pregnancy and avoid expenses the woman or the child might bring. But, he was quick to point out, Joseph would have been foolish to travel through the community with Charlotte at his side if he intended to murder her.

"Men are never wise when they resort to crime," retorted the prosecutor in his closing remarks.

When issuing instructions to the jury, the judge made sure to point out that Joseph had failed to provide an alibi, or even try to offer one, during the trial. Less than two hours later, the jury returned with a guilty verdict. They sentenced him to death.

Even after he was sentenced, Joseph maintained his innocence. Before he died, the doomed man apparently said he was taking Charlotte to another poorhouse when they stopped in the early morning for breakfast. In a fit of despair, she had thrown herself into the flames. Joseph said he couldn't save her. In fear of being blamed for her death, he said he covered Charlotte's body with debris before returning to the poorhouse.

On Joseph's execution day, February 8, 1881, about 1,000 people flocked to the jail yard in Annapolis Royal to attend his hanging. Hangings were no longer public spectacles in Nova Scotia, and the gallows were hidden behind a six-metre-high fence. Angered that they wouldn't be able to witness the punishment, the mob began pushing and shaking the fence, quickly knocking it over. In the adjoining courthouse, judges, reporters, and lawyers pressed against the window to watch the death sentence be carried out.

Although reports say Joseph paced the floor the night before his death, he seemed relaxed as the noose went around his neck. The throng of people, who had created mayhem earlier, reportedly uttered not a sound as the trap door opened and Joseph was hanged.

Chapter 8
Fluke of Evidence

ritish subjects were in a festive mood around the world. Queen Victoria was officially taking over the crown that day, June 28, 1838. It was a time for celebration and jubilation.

In Amherst, Nova Scotia, a parade was being organized, and the merriment was on the verge of moving into high gear. But as people gathered to celebrate, tragic news began to spread. There had been a murder in River Phillip, about 17 kilometres east of town. A farmer by the name of John Clem had been brutally attacked in his home, his housekeeper and her daughter badly injured.

The more people talked, the more they compared stories. The more they compared stories, the more speculation arose over who could have committed such a grisly act. Then someone mentioned they had met the farmer's hired hand, Maurice Doyle, earlier that day. Someone else mentioned how Maurice seemed to be in a rush. Yet another pointed out that he said he was heading to New Brunswick.

Meanwhile, in River Phillip, two of the farmer's neighbours, William Hussey and John Winsby, were still trying to get a grip on the horrendous discovery they had made.

Stopping by on business, William happened on a devastating scene. John Clem's face was battered. His head lay on a blood-drenched pillow. When he spoke, blood poured from his mouth.

There was more.

In the next room, red splotches covered the bedding. Clem's housekeeper, Elizabeth Pipes, and her 12-year-old daughter, Jane, lay seriously injured. Elizabeth lay on the bed with her forehead gashed open, talking senselessly. Her daughter's head rested in a puddle of blood, one of her teeth dangling from her open mouth.

Leaning over the pair to examine their injuries, William was startled by movement he caught out of the corner of his eye, at the doorway of the house. Fearful the attacker had returned, William quickly realized it was another neighbour. John Winsby had just walked in, also stopping by to do some business with Clem. He was just as shocked and terrified by the bloody scene.

Clem died only moments after his neighbours arrived.

River Phillip was a small, tight-knit rural community.

Secrets were hard to keep and easy to spread. Even though Clem lived in a rundown shack, people suspected that he wasn't a poor man, keeping large wads of cash in a trunk by his bed. As William and John took in the violent scene, they noticed pieces of the trunk scattered about. Only bits of junk were left — certainly no bundle of money.

Once word spread that Maurice Doyle was missing, the farmhand became the prime suspect. The justice of the peace decided to head up a search party and go after him. He and a man who said he could identify Maurice galloped off on horseback toward Sussex, New Brunswick, about 160 kilometres from Amherst, where they suspected Maurice was heading.

Maurice's apprehension was high drama. The suspect was just about to climb on board a stagecoach that was heading farther west. One of the men jumped him, bringing Maurice to the ground. They bound his hands with rope and searched his belongings, uncovering £25 (about $3,500 today). The 24-year-old Cape Bretoner seemed surprised when told his boss was dead.

Maurice's explanation for skipping town was simple. His brother was sailing out of Saint John any day, en route to the West Indies. Maurice just wanted to say goodbye. As luck would have it, Clem had fired Maurice the day before he died, leaving the farmhand free to travel. He had nothing but praise for Clem and acknowledged he was paid well for his work. But the two-man law enforcement team was convinced Maurice was lying.

Despite the lack of physical evidence, Maurice was charged with Clem's murder and taken to trial. The viciousness of the farmer's death and the savage attack on Elizabeth and her daughter stirred a tremendous amount of interest in Nova Scotia. When the trial began on September 25, the judge, Brenton Halliburton, had a difficult time reaching the courtroom because of the throng filling Amherst streets.

Inside, lawyer James F. Gray was getting ready for a challenging prosecution. He still had very little physical evidence linking Maurice to Clem's death and knew a conviction was iffy at best. He was, however, counting on some help from the defence lawyer, Charles Halliburton (no relation to the judge). The young lawyer had been practising for only a couple of years. Gray, with 12 years behind him, was hoping the inexperience would lead to a few mistakes.

Gray got what he'd hoped for. While cross-examining Crown witnesses, the defence lawyer inadvertently let them reveal that Maurice was a "drinking man" and that Clem had expressed concern about and dislike of his farmhand. These observations certainly didn't seal the conviction, but it was help Gray happily received.

The jury also learned that the farmer had died of a severe gash to his temple, which went five centimetres into his brain. More axe wounds covered his head and shoulders, they were told, and pieces of the trunk were scattered about the room. The murder weapon, its head covered in blood, was found outside Clem's house.

Gray had no other tangible evidence to present to the jury. No one had witnessed the attacks, so Maurice could not be placed at the scene. The attack happened in the early morning hours, before anyone was awake, so the woman and her daughter couldn't say who had wielded the axe and beat them. The only thing prosecutors could use against Maurice was his hasty departure out of town.

However, Gray's experience had taught him that what was missing in solid facts could often be compensated for with circumstantial evidence. That's what he based the rest of his case on, starting with John Sentorius's story.

Sentorius operated a small ferry that transported travellers across River Phillip. When he took the witness stand, he talked about his encounter with Maurice during the early morning hours before Clem's body was found. Maurice asked to borrow Sentorius's rowboat. The man agreed and watched as he paddled off into obscurity. After about four hours, Maurice returned and asked to be taken to the other side. But first, he went into Sentorius's home and changed his shirt.

As the men crossed the river in darkness, Maurice seemed to put his full trust in Sentorius. He explained that he owed money and was on the run because he couldn't pay up. Then he asked the rowboat operator to say they had crossed the river in the other direction if anyone were to ask about him. He also added he had been involved with a neighbouring farmer's daughter and was anxious to get out of town.

Maurice then got out of the boat and walked down the road toward Amherst, Sentorius told the jury.

When Sentorius heard of Clem's murder later in the day, he immediately went to find the shirt Maurice had shed in his kitchen in the night. On its sleeves, he found drops of blood.

Another witness, John Mulroy, testified about seeing the farmhand the night before Clem's death was discovered. Mulroy lived across River Phillip from Clem and said he thought nothing unusual about Maurice's visit that night. In hindsight, however, the accused man was asking too many questions and acting suspiciously, Mulroy testified. During the visit, Maurice asked when Mulroy had last seen Clem and whether he knew if Elizabeth Pipes was home.

One witness told about fixing Clem's red wallet several years earlier. Because he had no matching red leather, he'd used black instead, creating a distinctive case. A similar billfold had been found in Maurice's possession when he was apprehended in Sussex.

Elizabeth Pipes hadn't totally recovered from her vicious assault when she sat in the witness stand to testify against Maurice. She was still unable to identify her attacker. She did, however, identify the red and black wallet and tell of a threat the accused man once made to her — he'd said he would "cut my dammed head off when he would catch me alone."

Maurice provided little defence. In a statement to the jury, he only disputed Pipes's comments about the wallet, insisting it belonged to him. He shed no other light on the matter, gave no other explanation for some of his suspicious actions, and disputed no other testimony.

The jury left for deliberations armed with plenty of circumstantial evidence and only some physical evidence. Although there were still many questions and much speculation, the deliberations proved easy. The jury quickly returned with a guilty verdict.

Maurice appeared to have been relying on the circumstantial evidence working in his favour. He dropped his face into his hands and cried as the jury announced the decision. His sobs continued as the judge sentenced him to hang, adding his own moral lecture as part of the sentence. "Never, in the course of a long professional life, have I met with an instance of depravity equal to that with which you now stand convicted."

Two days later, on September 27, 1838, Maurice Doyle was sent to the gallows and hanged for the murder of John Clem.

Chapter 9
A Fiend in Human Shape

hen the *Saladin* left Valparaiso, Chile, in February 1844 bound for England, 14 people were on board. Three months later, when the ship was discovered run aground in Nova Scotia, only six seamen remained. In between, there had been a bloody, vicious battle for control.

Just two passengers were aboard the *Saladin* as it left Chile: Captain George Fielding and his 14-year-old son, also George. Captain Fielding was apparently fleeing Valparaiso after having escaped from jail. The former skipper of the English ship *Vitula* had been imprisoned for illicit trading. George, who had evaded capture, helped his father escape by bringing him a large cloak, a common garment worn in the area. Disguised as a native, Fielding walked out of the jail, past a guard, and on to freedom. The two hid at the docks for a few days before finding the *Saladin* and convincing her captain, Alexander McKenzie, to take them home to England.

Captain McKenzie was renowned for his strict and orderly ships. One crewman with 10 years' experience at sea said that McKenzie was "the most severe and dissatisfied master I ever sailed under." Fielding ran his ships in a similar manner. He was known as a bully who argued with his crews and fed them barely enough.

Now that he was a passenger, Fielding was in a different position, but he found it impossible to step away from the lead role. It wasn't long after the *Saladin* sailed that the two captains began to clash. At first, they were small yet insulting confrontations, usually instigated by Fielding. He would refuse to eat dinner with McKenzie, for example.

The conflicts soon escalated. Fielding openly criticized, contradicted, and cursed McKenzie in front of his crew. Afterward, he would rehash the argument with some crewmen, particularly the sail maker and cook, George Jones. At the same time, he openly fantasized about what he would do with some of the cargo on board.

The *Saladin* was laden with valuable freight. The 70 tonnes of copper, nearly a tonne of silver in the form of 13 bars, and trunks of coins added up to a small fortune. For a man like Fielding, who had nothing, such riches were too close to resist.

Shortly after the ship set sail from Chile, Fielding made

his first move. Sensing that Jones didn't like McKenzie's iron hand, he suggested mutiny to Jones, promising the sail maker he would become his right-hand man. Intrigued by Fielding and enticed by his dreams of riches, Jones readily agreed and took the idea to some of the crewmen.

To make sure McKenzie stayed in the dark about their plan, Fielding and Jones moved slowly and carefully. By mid-April, John Hazleton, William Trevaskiss, and Charles Gustavus Anderson were set to take part in the ship takeover, so Fielding put his plan into action.

Under the cover of darkness at sea, the ship's mate was startled from his sleep. Hazleton, Trevaskiss, and Anderson stood over him, axes poised. It took only two blows to kill the man. His body was then plunged into the sea.

Moving to the deck, the gang called for a watchman. As he surfaced and took the wheel, he too was attacked. Wielding their axes, they took their second victim, throwing his butchered body into the sea as well.

Next, the carpenter was called. Unaware of the violence that awaited him, the man was dealt a severe blow just as he surfaced from below deck. Stunned, but still alive, he was thrown overboard before he could gather his senses. The boat sailed away, leaving him in its wake, but his calls of "Murder!" sounded in the dark. Meant as a warning for the others on board, the carpenter's shouts only opened the opportunity for Fielding and his followers to truly take control of the ship.

As the carpenter's warnings rang out, some of Fielding's group called to the captain, telling him of the man overboard. McKenzie rose quickly from his bed and rushed to reach the deck. As he came on deck, he was giving the order to turn about. Instead, Anderson was waiting for him. He struck his captain with his fist. McKenzie reached to retaliate but was clearly outnumbered. There was a brief scuffle before the captain was restrained by Anderson and Jones.

Fielding was ready. Grabbing an axe, he repeatedly struck the helpless captain until he was dead. The gang tossed the mutilated body overboard. Fielding turned to his men and stated, "The ship is ours."

They sailed on.

Two other ship's officers became victims that night, one meeting death after being struck by an axe, the other dealt such a vicious blow that the force sent him tumbling overboard.

Throughout the night, Fielding's son sat quietly on the deck, watching.

The group, by a suggestion from Fielding, originally had two more victims in mind. But whether the passion for killing faded as night turned into morning or whether the men came to grips with the acts they had just committed, William Carr and John Galloway were spared. Instead, they were given an ultimatum: join the mutiny or die. The choice was obvious — they joined the mutineers.

The night of killings had worked up a hunger in the men, so Carr prepared a huge breakfast. As they ate, the men relived the night's events. Bellies full and egos inflated, they set about the job of raiding the ship. Money attached to letters for postage was removed; victims' trunks overturned; silver, copper, and coins stolen; and clothing of the dead men divided among the living.

Despite this alliance, there was no trust among the men — each knew he could be the next victim. Trying to ease one another's minds, they agreed to throw all weapons overboard, saving only one pistol to kill poultry during the remainder of the passage. Knives, axes, and hammers were also thrown into the sea.

In a final act of unity, the men took Fielding's Bible, then each laid on a hand and swore "to be brotherly together."

Apparently, the oath meant nothing to Fielding — his murderous thirst wasn't yet quenched. As he went about seeking more victims, his fickleness and lack of loyalty became glaringly obvious to the surviving crewmen. Fielding approached Galloway and suggested killing the others, except his son and Hazleton. That way, he explained, there would be more loot to share among fewer people.

When Galloway refused, Fielding presented the same idea to Anderson. Fielding was turned down again. This time, Anderson called his bluff. He told the rest of the crew about the proposed plan.

The self-appointed captain made another fatal mistake that day. He was careless. Two pistols he had saved from the purge were discovered, as was gun powder. The crew suspected that Fielding intended to turn the guns on them, and they weren't about to let that happen.

Fielding's game was up. The group quickly overtook their new leader, restraining him and keeping watch over him throughout the night.

"The captain was kept tied till morning," Trevaskiss later confessed. "And the men did not go to bed. We were afraid of him and kept his son from him, lest he should loose him."

Early the next morning, the men brought Fielding to the deck to decide what to do with him. Some suggested dropping him on the first piece of land they passed, but the mutinous captain had awakened the lust for killing in some of the crew.

Jones ordered Carr and Galloway to grab Fielding. Neither had taken part in any of the murders and were refusing to take part in this one as well. Putting their hands on Fielding, however, gave them direct involvement in the death. Feeling they had no choice but to obey the order, Carr and Galloway threw Fielding overboard. Then, following Jones's orders, they seized Fielding's son and threw him overboard, too.

Now only six aboard the *Saladin*, the crew continued with Fielding's plan to head toward the Gulf of St. Lawrence, scuttle the ship, take their share of the loot, and walk away. En route, they covered the ship's name and painted the head in an attempt to sail the ship into ambiguity.

One problem with killing all the officers and the extra

captain was finding someone qualified enough to sail the vessel. Anderson, deemed to be the most experienced, was put in charge. It's unclear whether it was his lack of experience that caused the *Saladin* to run aground in Country Harbour, in southeast Nova Scotia. But getting stuck certainly wasn't part of the master plan.

Still, there they were, stuck just southwest of Chedabucto Bay, which separates Cape Breton from the mainland. Residents onshore quickly made contact with the captain of a passing ship, who made his way to the vessel in distress. Tying a rope around his waste and relying on the *Saladin* crew to hold the other end, the captain made his way through the water to board the ship. He spent 35 hours on board, trying to sort out what happened and take inventory of the valuables. Sending word to the closest judge, he left the ship, nearly capsized.

Nova Scotia proved to be the end of the journey for the six men. A few days after the captain left them, Jones, Hazleton, Trevaskiss, Anderson, Carr, and Galloway were taken ashore. They arrived in leg irons on a Halifax dock in the spring of 1844.

Throughout their trials, held in June and July, the men offered details and admitted to their roles in the *Saladin* killings. Jones, Hazleton, Trevaskiss, and Anderson were found guilty of killing Captain McKenzie. Because of the guilty verdict and death sentence, the other charges were dropped. Carr and Galloway were acquitted of the charges of killing Captain Fielding and his son.

Whenever the men spoke of their time on the *Saladin*, they maintained the same common defence. Fear of Fielding made them turn against their captain and shipmates. During his trial, Trevaskiss called Fielding "that fiend in human shape," while one of the defence lawyers talked of Fielding corrupting the youthful crew. "Sad for them, even more than for himself, was the hour when he first breathed the temptation into their ears," the lawyer said. "They were all young men, with few traces of crime upon them; and it was possible, could any one suppose, for depravity comes by slow degrees, that they could have planned such a tragedy?"

But in his address to the Halifax jury, the judge instructed them to discount those worries. "A man is not justified in taking life, even if actually attacked, unless there be that degree of violence and peril to produce bodily fear," the judge said, adding it would have been just as easy to warn the others of the deadly plot as it was to take part in it.

On July 30, with a company of soldiers surrounding the scaffolding of the gallows to keep the crowds back, Jones, Hazleton, Trevaskiss, and Anderson were led to their death. The oldest was 23.

Moments before their death, the men turned to one another and said goodbye, kissing one another on the cheek and shaking hands. Jones then addressed the crowd, expressing his "deep sorrow" for the deed he committed and hoping God would pardon him. After the executioner lowered their hoods, the four trap doors were opened simultaneously.

Chapter 10
Revenge

leanor Power liked to daydream about the contents of the heavy oak chest her former boss stored in his home. She had once tried to open it, but the lid was locked. Whenever she had mentioned the chest to her boss, he acted strangely, quickly dismissing her questions. Eleanor reasoned the chest could only contain his fortunes.

William Keen's wealth was no secret. In 1754, the St. John's bigwig was a successful businessman — the largest fish trader in the region — and he had just been appointed magistrate. For two decades, he had been tirelessly campaigning the British government for tougher laws in the land. Now, he had the authority to judge criminal cases. With wealth and power, Keen was part of the government's inner circle.

As part of the upper class, Keen had several servants. Eleanor had been one of them, working as Keen's maid. She quit when she married Robert Power and settled down in the nearby fishing village of Freshwater Bay, where Robert worked at sea. Life was hard in the sea shanty. Eleanor often pondered Keen's wealth, locked away in the chest, and wondered about stealing it. All she needed to pull off the heist, she pointed out, were accomplices. There was no way she was strong enough to carry the heavy trunk full of money herself.

Her musings caught the interest of Edmund McGuire. A friend of the Power's, McGuire was also acquainted with Keen. In early 1754, Keen had convicted the soldier of assaulting a police officer. McGuire disputed the verdict, but to no avail. He was sentenced to nearly 24-hour-a-day confinement to his military compound and deportation from Newfoundland.

With McGuire's punishment, Keen lived up to his reputation for handing out tough sentences, especially to soldiers and sailors. He once sentenced a soldier to 20 days in jail and 21 lashes for stealing three potatoes, even though there had been no evidence to support the accusation.

Despite his sentence, McGuire had no problem plotting revenge against Keen with three fellow solders. John Munhall, Dennis Hawkins, and John Moody had also appeared before Keen and harboured vengeance toward the man. Over the next few months, the soldiers mulled over how to avenge their convictions.

Eleanor's idea of stealing the magistrate's fortune was

perfect. McGuire, practically tasting the sweet vengeance, leaped at Eleanor's suggestion — here, finally, was the plan he had been looking for. In the late summer of 1754, he began to plot the details. Robert was quickly on board, too. McGuire knew his pals from the garrison, Munhall, Hawkins, and Moody, would also be willing to take part. Soon, Eleanor and Robert's neighbours, Paul MacDonald, Lawrence Lamley, Nicholas Tobin, and Matthew Halluran, also fishermen, were in on the plot.

Throughout August 1754, the group met often to discuss how they would execute the robbery. During one meeting, they each placed their hands on a prayer book and swore allegiance to one another. In early September, the Freshwater Bay group rowed to St. John's and met the soldiers. The 10 proceeded to Keen's summer home, ready to commit the crime. But they were surprised to find fishermen nearby, cleaning the day's catch, so the robbery was put off.

A few days later, the group tried again. This time, they found two boats tied at the dock near Keen's summer home and knew he wasn't alone. Their plan was cancelled a second time.

On the night of September 9, the group made their final attempt. Again pledging loyalty to one another by swearing on a Bible, the gang broke into the house via the back entrance. Under the cover of darkness, as the others, armed with muskets, kept watch around the property, Eleanor, McGuire, Halluran, Lamley, Moody, and Munhall went into the home to search for the chest. Eleanor, dressed in men's clothing, led the group through the home she knew so well.

The trunk found, two of the men hoisted it up and others lit the way. As the treasure was carried outside, Lamley and Halluran crept silently through the home, laying chairs on their sides and opening drawers in the dining and living rooms. They were attempting to make the robbery look like a random act, rather than the orchestrated burglary it was. The two helped themselves to a few silver spoons before leaving the home.

Once everyone was outside, the group eagerly went into the nearby woods to crack open the chest. They were anxious to examine the fortune they would share. Although Eleanor had no way of knowing how much money Keen had stashed, she'd promised each gang member he would receive £1,000 (about $262,300 today) — a tidy sum in their eyes.

As McGuire struck the lock with the butt of his musket, the others stood back and watched breathlessly. He struck once, twice, then one last time. The catch crumbled. McGuire's thirst for revenge was nearly quenched. He could taste it now.

All 10 gang members gasped when the trunk's lid was opened. Instead of the gold coins and crisp bills they'd imagined, there was only liquor.

That was enough for most of them. They were ready to listen to fate. This was their third failed attempt at the robbery — it should have been an indication to ditch the plan and go home.

But McGuire was livid. Consumed by his vendetta against Keen, he told the group no one was leaving until they had some of the magistrate's money in their hands. If anyone attempted to abandon the plan, he seethed, he would kill them. McGuire's rage left no doubt in the minds of the others that he meant business — they weren't about to test him.

He laid out a new plan: everyone except Eleanor, whom he blamed for the bungled robberies, and Lamley would return to the house. Lamley's job was to make sure Eleanor didn't run off. The others would stake out the property and surrounding area as before. Halluran, Munhall, and Moody would accompany him inside to search for the money. If they couldn't find Keen's money on their own, they would demand that the magistrate tell them. If Keen refused, McGuire fumed, they would punish him. Halluran was the only one who spoke up to give McGuire his full support.

Back into the house they trod. McGuire and Halluran made their way to Keen's bedroom on the second floor. The others scoured the closets and cupboards on the main floor, looking for a money stash. As the magistrate slept, McGuire knelt on his knees and peered under the bed.

Sure enough, he found another wooden trunk.

But as McGuire dragged the trunk from its hiding place, the magistrate stirred from his sleep. When he got up to investigate, McGuire quickly threw a quilt over his head. Keen began to fight, extinguishing the candle McGuire was holding, causing Keen to struggle even more. In the confusion, Keen began to shout "Murder!"

Up to that point, Halluran had been watching the scene unfold. Now he began to strike the judge with a scythe. McGuire also inflicted a blow to Keen's head with the butt end of his musket. The magistrate fell to the floor, desperately injured but still alive.

The reality of the bloodied, battered man startled the two men. Leaving Keen in a heap, McGuire and Halluran went downstairs and out into the night, their fellow conspirators at their heels. The members of the group silently sneaked off, each in their own direction.

When Keen was found the next morning by a servant, the search for his attackers was on. Given his reputation as a ruthless judge, those who might have wanted to seek revenge were many. Unfortunately, the police officers available to investigate the crime were few. The military was called in to help, but because Keen had been hardest on soldiers in his courtroom, the very men investigating his death were considered prime suspects. Still, if the soldiers knew anything of the scheme their comrades had been involved in, they whispered not a word to investigators.

On September 29, Keen died of his injuries, and the police investigation stepped up. They'd failed to uncover any suspects after the robbery, but now a more concerted effort was made to find the murderers. Around the beginning of October, police began to knock on doors to ask questions.

When police rapped on Nicholas Tobin's door and asked if he knew anything about the crime against Keen, the man admitted he had some information. But, before uttering a word, Tobin insisted on immunity from trial. The police agreed.

Tobin proceeded to tell all. Thanks to his confession, on October 8, just over a week after Keen's death, the gang members faced trial. Only one hearing was held for all nine. Each was given the opportunity to testify and tell their side of the story. Eleanor and Robert uttered only that they were not guilty. McGuire ensured he implicated Halluran, admitting that the two of them had struck equal blows upon the magistrate.

Others begged for mercy. Moody asked to be sentenced to "transportation," meaning he would be sent out on the first ship travelling across the Atlantic. He had been a last-minute addition to the crew, he argued, joining in on the plot only just before it happened. The rest of the gang, acknowledging that too much of the truth had been revealed, pointed to Eleanor as the leader and main conspirator in the robbery.

Two doctors told the court that Keen had died of the wounds inflicted by the scythe and the butt end of the gun. With only Nicholas Tobin's testimony, the brief comments from the other gang members, and the doctors' statements, the jury began its deliberations.

Within half an hour, the jury returned with a verdict. All nine were guilty. Presiding judge Michael Gill sentenced them to be hanged. As added punishment for Edmund

McGuire and Matthew Halluran, the judge ordered they be "hanged in chains from some Publick Place," to be selected by the governor.

The governor, apparently having a sardonic sense of justice, announced that the hangings would happen two days later on Keen's own wharf — the same landing the gang had used to gain access to the magistrate's home. He then ruled that the bodies of McGuire and Halluran would be hung in the town centre.

The following day, Eleanor and Robert Power were executed at noon on the same gallows, hanged back to back. They were the first couple to be hanged together. Eleanor also had the distinction of being the first English Canadian woman to be hanged. As for the remaining five, they received a reprieve from their executions and were later pardoned by the king. They were, however, banished from Newfoundland.

Keen had fought most of his life for a formal justice system in Newfoundland. He finally got his wish. Ironically, his own murder trial was the first to be held in the new system.

Chapter 11
A Murderous Affair

atherine Snow and Tobias Mandeville were in love. They wanted to spend all their time together, but they had one problem — Catherine's husband, John.

Tobias was often at the Snow home, visiting with the family or helping John with clerical work for his fishing business. It wasn't a large business, but after fishing out of Harbour Grace for 20 years, John owned his own boat and was doing well enough to employ Tobias, Arthur Spring to help at sea, and Kit White to help Catherine at home. John's fishing trips left Catherine at home with the couple's seven children for long periods of time, so she welcomed Kit's help. Tobias was also around to help out if necessary.

Catherine's affair with Tobias started as a simple fling.

In 1833, Catherine was in her early 40s and apparently unhappy living the life of a fisherman's wife. Tobias, who was 25, showed considerable interest in Catherine. That spring, the two had a brief lustful encounter in the woods near the Snow home. Instead of a one-time rendezvous though, the meeting was the start of a deadly plot.

While Tobias and Catherine were falling head over heels in love, Arthur Spring was growing increasingly unhappy with his boss. He worked hard while on the fishing boat with John but felt his boss was taking advantage of him. Convinced John was cheating him out of fair wages, Arthur was vocal about his discontent. He complained to anyone who would listen, including Catherine and Tobias.

The pair was sympathetic to Arthur's grumbling. Well aware of their illicit affair, Arthur in turned showed some compassion for Tobias and Catherine's situation. As restlessness grew among the three, the plan to murder John was put into place. Murder, after all, was the only way to guarantee John would disappear for good. In order to secure Arthur's loyalty, the couple apparently promised to pay his back pay and increase his salary.

On August 31, Catherine's two oldest daughters, who were about 16 and 17, went down the road to a wake for a neighbour. Catherine had been to the wake earlier in the day, so Kit went with the girls. They expected it would be late before they returned home.

After the remaining five children were tucked into bed

for the night, Catherine gave one of her husband's shotguns to Arthur, shooing him off to the wharf. Her husband had made a quick jaunt across the bay to fetch Tobias and the two would soon be returning. It was Arthur's job to make sure that this was John's last trip across the bay, ever.

When the girls returned the next day, they wondered where their father was. Catherine told them he had gone fishing and wouldn't be back for a few days. Since he often went to sea for days at a time, it was a likely story — no one gave it a second thought.

But by September 5, when John's fellow fishermen noticed he'd been gone longer than usual, they began to talk. They reported his absence to police, and officials organized a small search along the shores. Five days later, after still no sign of John, a full-scale rescue effort was launched. Fifty men in eight boats dragged the harbour, but hope was dim. They knew these waters. They knew that if John had indeed tumbled into the water, the dogfish, a small sharklike creature that was plentiful off the coast of Newfoundland at the time, would have consumed his remains by now.

Catherine, meanwhile, was nonchalant about John's disappearance. She confirmed to police that Tobias and Arthur had helped search for her husband, but she was insistent he was still out to sea, fishing. Perhaps, she suggested, John had had an accident at sea.

As time progressed, foul play passed through the minds

of authorities. They began to ask questions around town, look for witnesses, and retrace John's last known steps. It was soon discovered that Tobias had been picked up by his boss on August 31. Police also learned about Arthur's unhappiness with his job. On October 5, more than a month after John's disappearance, Arthur was arrested on suspicion of murder. Tobias was brought in later that day.

The men confirmed police suspicions. John Snow was dead. They agreed on very little else, and their accounts of John's death turned into a game of finger pointing. Tobias was quick to tell police that Arthur had done the deed alone. He claimed that he was first off the boat, with John right behind him. He stepped out of the way to give Arthur, standing at the other end of the dock, plenty of room to shoot the boss.

Arthur told a different story. He said he didn't have the heart to pull the trigger when it came time, so he dropped the gun and fled. Arthur said Tobias then picked up the weapon and fired the fatal shot.

However, there were two other details the men agreed on: the disposal of John's body and Catherine's involvement. Both Tobias and Arthur told police how they had tied up the body with rope, lowered it into the water, and towed it into the bay. There, they fastened the rope to a small anchor and threw it overboard. They also revealed how Catherine had cooked up the whole plan. She'd encouraged them to kill her husband and helped them commit the crime, they told police.

Tobias also admitted to his affair with Catherine, saying

they had even been together the night John was killed. Kit later confirmed the story — she had found his pants beside Catherine's bed the next day.

Catherine didn't stick around to find out what happened to Tobias and Arthur. Leaving her children with Kit, Catherine was gone by the time police went to her home to hear her version of the ordeal. A province-wide police search began. Officials questioned her friends, hoping they would discover that one of them was hiding the woman. After a week, Catherine was indeed found at a friend's home nearby.

She knew nothing, she claimed, of any plot to kill her husband. Instead, Catherine told police she had given the loaded gun to Arthur to shoot some stray dogs that had been causing problems at the dock. When Arthur and Tobias arrived back at her home and she asked about her husband, they apparently told her he would arrive soon.

Catherine maintained her innocence throughout the investigation, never wavering from her claim of ignorance of the ploy. Police didn't believe her story, however. She was charged with accessory before the fact of murder. Tobias Mandeville and Arthur Spring were each charged with the murder of John Snow.

The intrigue of the love triangle and the depth of Catherine's involvement captured the curiosity of St. John's residents. They packed the courtroom on January 10, 1834, hoping to hear more details of the love affair, the slaying, and the woman's role.

The prosecuting lawyer had statements from Tobias and Arthur implicating each other in John's death, yet he acknowledged that the evidence against Catherine was circumstantial. The lawyer did, however, point to her blasé reaction to her husband's disappearance and the fact that she'd deserted her children.

Witness Mark Henneberry testified he had met Catherine just after Arthur was arrested. She was heading out of town and asked him to get word to Tobias and Arthur, reminding them to keep their mouths shut.

Although circumstantial, there was enough evidence to cast suspicion on Catherine. The judge, Chief Justice Henry John Boulton, noted the facts implicating Catherine in her husband's death and urged the jury, "I ask you to pay close attention to the circumstantial evidence against Catherine Snow. If you do not consider it conclusive, then give her the benefit of the doubt."

The jury was quick to reach its decision, deliberating for only 30 minutes. Arthur Spring, Tobias Mandeville, and Catherine Snow were all found guilty and sentenced to death.

But Catherine's lawyer had a surprise that shocked the courtroom — his client was pregnant. The next day, a jury of matrons gathered to examine Catherine. They reported to the judge that she was indeed "quick with child and in an advanced stage." A reprieve was granted on her execution.

Tobias's and Arthur's executions went ahead as

scheduled, though. Only three days after being convicted, they were hanged.

In the months following the trial, priests in the area worked to exonerate Catherine. Public sentiment was that the evidence from the trial raised more questions than it answered and the woman was a victim of circumstances. The clergy circulated a petition denouncing the jury's verdict and calling on the court to overturn the decision.

Unfortunately, few residents were willing to sign their names to the petition. They may not have believed she had anything to do with her husband's death, but they weren't impressed with her adulterous relationship. The petition was rejected.

After the birth of her eighth child, Catherine fell ill. Oddly, authorities decided to continue the reprieve of her death sentence until she was feeling better. Finally, on July 22, 1834, a healthy Catherine prepared for her death.

According to the custom of the day, corpses were buried in drab clothing. In the name of efficiency, Catherine was dressed in these clothes before going to the gallows. She apparently went hysterical when she saw herself in a mirror, dressed for the grave.

Once calmed by a priest, she made her way to the scaffold. Catherine maintained her innocence even as the noose was placed around her neck. "I was a wretched woman but as innocent of any participation in the crime of murder as an unborn child," she said.

Typically, Catherine's body would have been hung in a public square as a deterrent to others before she was buried in the prison cemetery. But the priests who had tried to save her won the fight to have the spectacle rescinded. Instead, Catherine was allowed to be buried in the Roman Catholic graveyard.

She was the last woman hanged in Newfoundland.

Further Reading

Fitzgerald, Jack. *Ten Steps to the Gallows.* St. John's, NF: Jesperson Press, 1981.

Grant, B. J. *Six for the Hangman.* Fredericton, NB: Fiddlehead Books and Goose Lane Editions, 1983.

Hornby, Jim. *In the Shadow of the Gallows. Criminal Law and Capital Punishment in Prince Edward Island, 1769–1941.* Summerside, PEI: Institute of Island Studies, 1998.

Jobb, Dean. *Bluenose Justice.* Porters Lake, NS: Pottersfield, 1993.

Keeton, G. W., and John Cameron, eds. *The Veronica Trial.* Great Britain: William Hodge and Company Ltd., 1952.

Soucoup, Dan. *Looking Back.* Halifax, NS: Maritime Lines, 2002.

Stewart, James. *The Trials of George Frederick Boutelier and John Boutelier.* Halifax, NS: John Howe, 1791.

Acknowledgments

The author wishes to acknowledge the following additional sources for their assistance with the manuscript: *A Dance with Death*, by Frank W. Anderson; *New Brunswick Sea Stories*, by Dorothy Dearborn; *Uncertain Justice, Canadian Women and Capital Punishment 1754–1953*, by Murray F. Greenwood and Beverley Boissery; *Judges of New Brunswick and Their Times*, by Joseph Wilson Lawrence; *Lectures on the History of Newfoundland 1500–1830*, by Keith Matthews; *A Seaport Legacy — The Story of St. John's, Newfoundland*, by Paul O'Neill; *A History of Newfoundland and Labrador*, by Frederick W. Rowe; *The Murder of Charlotte Hill and the Trial and Hanging of Joseph Nicholas Thibault*, compiled by the Milford and Area Community Association. Further research also came from numerous magazine and newspaper accounts.

Thank you to all who helped in various ways in the creation of this book. Earlier writers of these stories blazed a trail to guide me. Some of you shared your knowledge, opinions, and research skills. Others helped out with various projects when I was madly trying to meet deadlines. Then there were those who spoke a gentle "You can do it" when they knew I needed to hear those words the most.

Specifically, thanks to members of the Periodical Writers

Association of Canada for your thoughts and advice whenever I asked. Thanks as well to the executive of the Canadian Farm Writers Federation for picking up the slack when I spent more time on murder writing than farm writing.

To the staff at the Moncton Public Library, the Milford and Area Community Association, and Glenda Dawe of the Centre for Newfoundland Studies at Memorial University, thank you for your assistance and patience.

Colleagues Heather Jones and Kevin Hursh, this would not have been possible without your understanding and flexibility. You have my deepest appreciation.

Thanks to Jill Foran and Lori Burwash for your excellent editing skills and to Altitude for this amazing opportunity.

My dear friend Debby Landry, you shared your wisdom with me and helped me see each story in a new light. For this, and for every single laugh we've shared over the years, you have my gratitude and sincere respect.

Thank you to all my family as well. Olivia and Mark, you're the best. And, Dale, thank you for your quiet surety and pride (and for doing all the dishes while I was writing).

I feel the need for special acknowledgment of the victims in these stories. Each died a tragic death, and I've tried to tell their stories with the utmost respect. I hope their souls are at peace.

About the Author

Allison Finnamore began her freelance journalism career in 2001 as a daily newspaper correspondent, spending countless hours covering all kinds of court proceedings, including murder trials. While working in the heartland of New Brunswick's potato belt, writing about farming also became an unavoidable pleasure. Allison writes primarily about agriculture and agri-business now but still has a keen interest in what goes on inside the courtrooms of Atlantic Canada.

Amazing Author Question and Answer

What was your inspiration for writing about East Coast murders?

Certainly, curiosity was a huge motivator. I've spent many hours covering all types of trials for daily newspapers, including murder trials. I always wonder about the people facing the charges and what circumstances in their lives brought them to that moment. Sometimes there was the opportunity to find out.

What surprised you most while you were researching East Coast murders?

I wasn't expecting there to be scads of killings, but I was surprised at how few there actually were. When I began my research, I started asking friends throughout Atlantic Canada for ideas of amazing murder stories in their provinces. Several people, especially in Newfoundland and Prince Edward Island, told me there haven't been many murders in their province — that they're reasonably quiet places. My friend Debby Landry, who is a criminologist, pointed out to me that Canada has one of the lowest homicide rates in the world. Crime rates are even lower on the East Coast.

What do you most admire about the person or people in this Amazing Story?

In the story about the death of John Clem, I developed a great respect for Elizabeth Pipes and her daughter. The two females were savagely beaten with an axe, yet managed to survive. Although they testified against the accused, Maurice Doyle, they were unable to tell any details of consequence. Still, I imagine those women relived the horror of that beating every day for the rest of their lives. That kind of strength and courage astounds me.

What escapade do you most identify with?

While I condone none of the killings, there are some instances where I can identify with why the murderers acted the way they did, facing the circumstances they did at the time. For instance, I can understand May Bannister fighting tooth and nail to make a better life for her children. I can see how Harry Flohr, when forced to choose between dying a brutal death or participating in the bloody mutiny, decided to assist with the murders on board the *Veronica*.

What difficulties did you run into when researching East Coast murders?

Some stories were easy to find out about. They've been told and recounted many times and, in some parts of Eastern Canada, have become folklore. The tale of Minnie McGee is an example of this — there's even a play based on Minnie. Other stories were a mere mention in history books and were far more challenging to research. That broad spectrum, from readily available material to information found only after many hours of digging, was a surprise. But the challenge of tracking down information is the fun part.

What part of the writing process did you enjoy most?

I love words. Once the story was dug up, the research was compiled, and I had the characters and story mapped out, my favourite part was sitting at the computer and writing my own version of the story, playing with words as I went.

Which other Amazing Stories would you recommend?

I loved *Strange Events* by Johanna Bertin and *The Black Donnellys* by Nate Hendley. Hélèna Katz's *The Mad Trapper* is next on my reading list.

Amazing Places to Visit

Maison Historique Pascal-Poirier
Art Gallery and Museum

399 Main Street, Shediac, NB

This heritage house, built in 1825, is one of the oldest buildings in the town and is dedicated to the life and work of Pascal Poirier, a descendant of Pascal Poirier, who helped transport Amasa Babcock from the Shediac area to the jail in Dorchester in 1805.

Woodleigh Replicas

Route 234, Burlington, just north of Kensington, PEI
(open seasonally)

Thirty large-scale replicas of castles and legendary buildings span the site, intermingling with English gardens and cool fountains. The site is the former homestead of William Millman's family, the young man who, in 1887, discovered he was going to be a father much sooner than he would have liked, then, panic-stricken, put an end to the matter once and for all.

St. John's, NF, Old St. John's

The Women's History Group at Memorial University has compiled a self-guided walking tour through the historical streets of St. John's. Divided into two parts, the Military Road Area and the Waterfront Area, each takes about an hour, with the Waterfront Area tour picking up at the end of the Military Road Area tour. A map and details of the attractions along the route are available at www.heritage.nf.ca/society/womenswalk/default.html.

Part of the Waterfront Tour includes a stop at the historic St. John's Courthouse, the site where Catherine Snow was hanged in 1834 after being found guilty of killing her husband, John. As well, the tour notes the location where Eleanor and Robert Power were hanged in 1754 for their part in the robbery and murder of magistrate William Keen.

OTHER AMAZING STORIES

These titles are available wherever you buy books. If you have trouble finding the book you want, call the Altitude order desk at **1-800-957-6888**, e-mail your request to: **orderdesk@altitudepublishing.com** or visit our Web site **at www.amazingstories.ca**

New AMAZING STORIES titles are published every month.